The Little Dog
Activity Book

Deborah Wood

tfh

T.F.H. Publications, Inc.

The Little Dogs' Activity Book

Project Team
Editor: Heather Russell-Revesz
Copy Editor: Joann Woy
Design: Mary Ann Kahn

T.F.H. Publications
President/CEO: Glen S. Axelrod
Executive Vice President: Mark E. Johnson
Publisher: Christopher T. Reggio
Production Manager: Kathy Bontz

T.F.H. Publications, Inc.
One TFH Plaza
Third and Union Avenues
Neptune City, NJ 07753

07 08 09 10 1 3 5 7 9 8 6 4 2

Library of Congress Cataloging-in-Publication Data
Wood, Deborah, 1952-
   The little dogs' activity book : fun and frolic for your fit four-legged friend / Deborah Wood.
      p. cm.
   Includes index.
   ISBN-13: 978-0-7938-0603-4 (alk. paper) 1. Games for dogs. 2. Dog sports. 3. Dogs—Exercise.
I. Title.
   SF427.45.W66 2007
   636.7'089371—dc22
   2006024693

This book has been published with the intent to provide accurate and authoritative information in regard to the subject matter
within. While every precaution has been taken in preparation of this book, the author and publisher expressly disclaim responsibility
for any errors, omissions, or adverse effects arising from the use or application of the information contained herein. The techniques
and suggestions are used at the reader's discretion and are not to be considered a substitute for veterinary care. If you suspect a
medical problem consult your veterinarian.

The Leader In Responsible Animal Care For Over 50 Years!™
www.tfh.com

Table of Contents

Introduction

Are you living with a desperate housedog? If you have a lap-sized dog, the chances are he's spending too much time on your lap. He probably doesn't get the exercise he needs, and the odds are that he doesn't use his brain as much as he'd like to, either.

In short, your portable-sized pooch is bored, bored, bored.

Little dogs have been big news for the last several years. It only makes sense: Small dogs fit into our busy, urban, mobile lifestyle better than do their larger cousins. If you live in an apartment or a condo, a dog under of about 20 (9 kg) pounds happily adjusts to your down-sized living space. If you like to travel, you can put your little guy into a carrier and fly across the country—or even around the world—together. If you're at retirement age, you know it's a lot easier to take care of the needs of a smaller dog rather than a larger one.

We share the rhythms of our lives with our canine companions (and it's one of the best deals we humans ever made). Unfortunately, it isn't always such a good deal for the dog. After all, your pint-sized pooch has all the same instincts and intelligence of a regulation-sized canine. Even if he's got a flat little face, paws the size of dimes, and likes to ride around in a purse, he still shares the ancient DNA of his wolf ancestors.

Your little dog needs to stretch and exercise his brain and his body. He needs the joy of using his nose to find things, chasing things that move, and playing with other dogs.

In short, your Lhasa Apso should have as much fun as a Labrador; a Chihuahua wants to experience as much life as a Collie; and a Miniature Pinscher deserves the same respect that people give to a Doberman Pinscher.

Desperate Housedogs

Happily, it's easy to do. Although your dog needs the same mental and physical challenges the big dogs enjoy, you can do it in a small space. You don't need 10 acres and a herd of sheep to keep your dog happy. Your living room can become the small-dog equivalent of Disneyland. You can even watch TV while you give him an aerobic workout.

Let this book be your guide. We've listed ideas and activities for every dog—and every human. If you or your dog aren't athletes, don't worry. There are still great things for you to do. Do you have a little speed demon? This book is chock-full of activities that will make his busy little heart sing. Or, if you're not so perfectly matched, and you're a high-energy person with a low-energy dog, we've got you covered, too.

I promise that the activities in this book will bring you closer than you can imagine to your dog. It will also help your dog to live a longer, healthier life. Humans who keep physically active and do challenging mental activities (such as crossword puzzles) are less likely to develop Alzheimer's disease, and dogs are no different. Pooches who are mentally and physically active are less susceptible to the doggie equivalent: canine cognitive dysfunction.

You already love your little dog. The ideas in this book are designed to get the two of you thinking as a team. Once you find the right activity, you're sure to laugh more often, and your little dog will respond with an unmistakable doggie grin. Your lives together will be more joyful than ever. And, at the end of the day, when he's contentedly snuggled in your lap, we've even included some doggie-themed puzzles for you to solve.

Let's get started and have some fun!

Part 1

Hangin' At Home: Having Fun Without Leaving the Hous

Chapter 1

Ask Yourself:
Built for Comfort or Built for Speed?

"I am built for comfort, I'm not built for speed…"—so goes lines in one of my favorite Hoyt Axton songs. As someone who's definitely built more for comfort, I can relate to the lyrics! And just like people, some dogs are more athletic and have higher energy levels than others. Some are "built for comfort," and some are "built for speed." When you understand your dog's physical and mental characteristics, you'll also figure out what makes him happy. When you provide that for him, you will have a partnership with your dog that will be the source of pride and joy for a lifetime.

Some games in this book every dog can play, like the Nose Games in Chapter 2. But other activities aren't so universal. It's important to look at things from your dog's point of view as you decide which activities are right for him.

What's Right for My Little Dog?

Ask yourself the following questions to help determine what type of little dog you have.

Is Your Little Dog Bored?

A bored dog is yappy, often destructive, and may amuse himself by playing "keep away" games with you. That's no fun for either of you. If you don't find activities that challenge this dog mentally and physically, you'll never know the bond that you could have had.

It's Somewhat Conditional Love

You know the mantra: Dogs give us unconditional love. But I believe that's a lie. Dogs have their own needs. When we ignore them, dogs are less happy—and less bonded to us—than when we meet their needs. Find activities right for your little dog, and you're sure to have a contented companion for life.

A barking dog may be a bored dog—keep him active!

Possible Activities

Bored dogs need activities. Really bored dogs need lots of activities! Keep these dogs occupied with plenty of exercise. Start the day with a long walk, or at least a rousing game of living room fetch. Make sure he's got interactive toys to entertain him when you're not home. Teach him tricks to keep his clever mind occupied.

Is Your Little Dog Shy?

Your dog might need a boost of confidence. These dogs need you to make them feel safe and secure. If a shy dog has too many demands placed on him, he'll withdraw into his own world. He'll learn to be afraid of you. While the bored dog needs stimulation, the shy dog must be

Exposing your shy dog to activities can help him overcome his fears.

taught skills slowly and gently. Do that, and you'll have a bond of trust beyond description.

Possible Activities

Shy dogs love games with rules. Once they understand the rules, they have the structure to relax and have fun. Think about obedience classes (positive methods only, of course) for your shy dog. Also, the organized fun and excitement of agility has brought a lot of shy dogs out of their shells. Just hanging out with a confident, happy, bold dog can help a shy dog blossom.

How Active Is Your Breed?

This chart is a good starting place to help you think about what activities your breed might enjoy.

Activity Level—High

These dogs need daily stimulation and vigorous exercise. Some will be able to play fetch for an hour inside, but others will need high-energy exercise such as agility or even jogging. These dogs usually make their own fun if you don't provide it for them—and that isn't always a pretty picture!

BREEDS

Affenpinschers
Australian Terriers
Bichons Frise
Border Terriers
Cairn Terriers
Cardigan Welsh
 Corgis

Jack Russell Terriers
Parson Russell
 Terriers
Miniature Pinschers
Miniature Poodles
Papillons
Pembroke Welsh
 Corgis

Rat Terriers
Schipperkes
Scottish Terriers
Shetland Sheepdogs
Silky Terriers
Smooth Fox Terriers
Toy Manchester
 Terriers

FAVORITE ACTIVITIES

Chase and fetch games, agility, flyball, hiking

High Energy:
Jack Russell Terrier

Moderate Energy:
Chihuahua

Low Energy:
French Bulldog

Activity Level—Moderate

These breeds typically adapt easily to the activity levels of their households. Their owners must take the initiative to make sure they stay active and healthy.

BREEDS

Beagles
Boston Terriers
Cavalier King
  Charles Spaniels
Chihuahuas
Chinese Cresteds
Dachshunds

Havanese
Italian Greyhounds
Maltese
Manchester Terriers
Miniature
  Schnauzers
Norfolk Terriers

Norwich Terriers
Pomeranians
Pugs
Skye Terriers
West Highland
  White Terriers
Yorkshire Terriers

FAVORITE ACTIVITIES

Long walks, dancing with dogs, tricks

Activity Level—Low

These dogs would happily live their lives as a pillow. While they usually won't be happy doing serious dog sports, and definitely aren't jogging partners, they need exercise and stimulation, too. They'll live much longer, happier lives if they get out of the house and have some fun!

BREEDS

Brussels Griffon
English Toy
  Spaniels

French Bulldog
Japanese Chin
Lhasa Apso

Pekingese
Shih Tzu
Tibetan Spaniels

FAVORITE ACTIVITIES

Therapy dogs, shorter walks (be prepared to carry or take the dog in a stroller for longer walks)

Is He More Body Than Leg?

For some dogs, the spirit is willing, but the flesh can't comply. For example, you may be active but own a dog who isn't designed for a jog (like the Pekingese). Ask this dog to do too much physical work, and he'll avoid you so he won't have to deal with what he can't do.

Is Your Dog "Verbally Gifted?"

Little dogs are notorious barkers, but maybe he's trying to tell you something. One reason a lap dog becomes a "yap dog": He's bored! Barking is a way of entertaining himself. Rather than getting frustrated with your verbally gifted pooch, think about activities for him to do.

Possible Activities

This dog still needs gentle exercise. If your walks are longer than he can handle, figure out a way to take him with you in a stroller or backpack. Play games with him. He might not fetch a stick across a field, but he might love to fetch a toy-dog-sized ball across the living room.

This dog also wants lap time. If you're a busy person, it's a signal to you that it's also important to sit still sometimes. Let him snuggle and cuddle while you read a book together. Read the funnies out loud to him. Pay attention to what makes your little guy feel good. Give him massages, and he'll follow you to the ends of the earth.

How Old Is Your Little Dog?

Those of us with smaller dogs are lucky: Most little dogs live longer, healthier lives than do their full-sized canine counterparts. Many small dogs are still active well into their teen years. Still, we all slow down as we age, and dogs are no exception. Like humans, moderate activity—both physical and mental—improves your dog's quality of life immensely.

No magic age defines "senior." Just as some people are running marathons at 65 while others are ready for a rocking chair, some dogs become sedate and sedentary at age 8 or so, while others are still competing in agility at age 13. Observe your dog to see if he's comfortable with his level of activity. If the dog who used to leap with joy at a jog now hangs back at the end of the leash, adjust his activity level.

And about the expression "You can't teach an old dog new tricks"—that was written about humans. Old dogs love to learn new things.

Possible Activities

If your dog used to go jogging, consider slowing down and walking with him. Take a dancing with dogs class. You design the routine to match your dog's abilities, so he gets to do what he does well, and doesn't have to attempt things that aren't comfortable for him. You could also take a tricks class. Show those young whippersnappers in the class that your old dog can, too, learn new things!

Beware of Canine Profiling

Although it can be helpful to consider your dog's breed when you're thinking about what kind of activities suit him, remember that each dog is an individual. The chart on pages 10 and 11 is just a general guide—it's important to observe your own dog and determine just how active he really is before you decide what to pursue.

A Japanese Chin taught me that important lesson. Chin are wonderful little dogs who seem to be chuckling at the world. Usually, they're the epitome of the total lap breed, with absolutely no interest in moving faster than a slow

Dog's like the Pekingese arem't built for speed.

stroll. But to every rule there is always an exception. One of the cleverest—and speediest—dogs I ever taught in an obedience class was a Japanese Chin.

I was in total shock when this dog zoomed to her owner on the "Come" command instead of ambling like most Chin do. This high-energy dog was the star in a class that included traditionally obedient breeds like Papillons and a Miniature Poodle.

The uniqueness of every dog should never be forgotten!

A Tale of Three Papillons

Understanding and fulfilling your dog's individual needs is something I learned from my own three Papillons: one a high-energy dog, one a moderate-energy dog, and one (at 15 years old) now a low-energy dog. Each one needs something—and receives something—different in their relationships with me.

The High-Energy Dog

The Energizer Bunny has nothing on my Pogo. This dog must have a point at which he tires out, but I just haven't found it yet. To satisfy his boundless energy, Pogo participates and titles in advanced obedience, takes tricks classes, is a certified therapy dog (who at age 2 was already regularly visiting kids in a

Dogs are individuals—some breeds you'd never suspect are great at sports like agility!

Tailor activities to your dog's needs.

hospital), works as my demo dog when I teach classes, and often comes with me when I give speeches or appear as a guest on a local television show. Oh— did I mention he practices his obedience at least three times a week?

The trick to handling my high-energy dog was not to be frustrated by him, but give him a wide variety of things to do—and make it exciting for him to perform his many tasks. He adores me because I give him a varied, interesting, intense, high-voltage life that suits his big personality.

The Moderate-Energy Dog

Radar is the Papillon who makes me look smart. He's a thinking dog who loves to please. When he was younger, he was a high-energy dog and excellent at obedience. At age 11, Radar has developed some chronic health problems. He's slowed down and no longer enjoys the rigors of competitive obedience. Still, he's not ready to retire from fun!

My job with Radar is to find things for him to do that use his clever brain but don't put too much stress on his body. Instead of obedience, his current class is dancing with dogs (also called canine freestyle). This activity is the best yet for keeping his interest up and his physical stress low. We select which tricks to do as we choreograph a routine to music. It's the perfect activity for him.

The Low-Energy, Senior, Shy Dog

My Papillon Goldie is not really a dog: She's a fairy princess who came to earth in the cutest costume available that day. I got her when she was a frightened, shivering 2-year-old who shook violently every time she left my house. She didn't stop shaking until she came back.

Gentle obedience training helped Goldie gain confidence, but she still needed lots of repetition to feel comfortable. My bond with Goldie was established by me practicing the same behaviors and giving her the same words over and over…and over and over.

She's gone from a moderate-energy dog to a low-energy one—right about the time she turned 14. She still enjoys walks, but can't go far. I bought a pet stroller so that she could join the other dogs on our walks. Most of her one-on-one time is on my lap, being gently held, and receiving the healing techniques of Tellington Touch (for more information check out the Resources). Our relationship is based on me being safe and predictable.

Goldie, Pogo, and Radar—3 Pappillons with different activity needs.

Get out and start having fun with your little guy.

I must treat each of my dogs as an individual; otherwise, each one of them would miss out on something they need. And I would miss out on all the joy I get from our relationship together.

Time to Get Started!

Think about your individual dog and what makes him happy, then read the chapters ahead. This book has dozens of things to do with your dog, and plenty that will suit your dog's needs. Pick those activities that bring both of you pleasure!

Dogs don't ask a lot of us, but they do need us to pay attention. Select the right activity for your dog, and you'll be rewarded with a wonderful two-way relationship (just like Lassie and Timmy).

What Every Dog "Nose":

Chapter 2

Scent Games for Your Little Dog

Nothing is more joyful to your dog than finding something with his nose. Every single dog on the planet loves to play scent games.

Even if you're not ready to tackle any of the other games in this book, the simple nose games in this chapter are a great way to start getting active with your dog. Other activities, like agility, require a certain level of physical fitness from your dog. Or they may require a large time commitment, like choreographing a dance routine for canine freestyle. And not everyone is the kind of party animal who enjoys inviting all the other little dogs over for a play date.

But nose games are different. Those in this chapter are universal. Do you have an active dog? Playing nose games will use his brain and tire him out as much as physical activity. Do you have a shy or worried dog? Nose games are great confidence builders. Do you have a puppy who isn't ready for serious training? Young pups can play these games as well as an adult. Do you have an old dog? Not a problem—scent is the one sense that almost never diminishes with age.

How a Dog's Nose Knows

Humans relate to the world primarily through our amazing gift of speech. Our memories are usually formed in words—a running narrative of the stories of our lives. Dogs, on the other hand, relate to the world primarily through their amazing gift of scent. Smell is a puppy's first sense. Your dog used his sense of smell to find his mom's milk before his eyes or ears were functioning, and he won't stop using his nose for his entire lifetime.

We really don't know quite why a dog's nose is so talented. The design is part of it. Experts say that a dog's nose is somewhere between 1,000 times and 10 million times more sensitive than a human's. (There's quite a range to that estimate, which proves just how much we still don't know about dogs' noses.) Dogs have up to 220 million scent cells, compared to about 5 million in humans. In dogs, the scent cell membranes are folded together in the nose; if they were smoothed out, they might cover an area larger than the dog's body.

Differences also exist in the way humans and dogs smell. Current thinking posits that humans smell things all in a jumble, and dogs smell each individual ingredient. So, when we sniff the odor of chicken soup on the stove, we react to the way the ingredients combine together. We think, "Oh yeah! Mom's famous soup for dinner tonight!"

Experts say that a dog's nose is somewhere between 1,000 times and 10 million times more sensitive than a human's.

Most experts believe that dogs smell each tiny ingredient individually. Your dog smells the chicken, the celery, the rice, the oregano, the salt, and each separate ingredient. (He may still be thinking, "Oh yeah! Mom's famous soup for dinner tonight!"—but he'll know more specifics about what's in that soup.)

One great thing about the way dogs' noses work is that size doesn't matter much. Small dogs can be just as good at scent games as big ones. Your flat-faced Pug or Pekingese can find objects by scent just as a German Shepherd Dog or a Basset Hound can. In fact, Beagles and Dachshunds—two proud members of the little dog contingent—are among the best scent-workers of any breed.

Living Room Scent Games

You can play these simple games with your dog to increase his brainpower, decrease his boredom, and strengthen his bond with you.

Game #1: Which Hand?

This game is not only easy, it's a great way to bond and have fun.

What You'll Need

Small treats

How to Play

* Close your fist around a little treat.
* Hold both hands out, and ask your dog "Which hand?"
* When he sniffs the correct hand, open up your hand and let him take the treat, telling him he's a little "nose genius."
* If he sniffs the wrong hand, just ignore him.
* Soon he'll learn to find the right one on the first sniff.

What does this simple exercise do? It makes him think! It allows him to use his most primal instinct—hunting with his nose—to get a treat from you.

Positively Obedient

Please forget the notion that "training" and "force" are synonymous. Modern dog training, especially for our little guys, should be fun for both of you. You don't need to be violent or raise your voice to be a leader to your dog. Just reward him when he's doing something right, and he'll go to the ends of the Earth to please you.

It's never a good idea to use force in dog training—and it can be downright dangerous if you try force on your pint-sized dog. A small dog's delicate throat can be permanently damaged with the jerk of a collar. His spine and hips can be seriously injured if you push him into a "sit" or "lie down" position.

Studies have consistently shown that dogs who get treat rewards learn faster, and retain more, than do dogs who are trained with force and threats. You like it when you get a paycheck for a job well done; your dog likes it when he gets a treat for a job well done!

Remember the newspaper technique: If you find yourself losing your temper and wanting to yell, calmly roll up a newspaper and hit yourself over the head, saying, "Bad human! No!"

Game #2: The Shell Game

This game is based on the same instincts as "Which Hand" but is a little more sophisticated. (And, of course, you and your dog are sophisticated.) This game is fun for your dog and makes great entertainment for your family and friends.

What You'll Need

* Three cups. You'll need lightweight cups that allow scent to waft through, so paper cups are best for this exercise.
* Treats

How to Play

* Line all three cups up on the floor.
* Make a big production of putting the treat under one cup—let him see what you've done.
* Tell your dog, "Find it!"
* When he indicates that the treat is under the cup, let your little canine Einstein have the treat.

❋ If your dog doesn't find the treat on the first try, show him where the treat is, and say "Find it!" again. Since he just saw the treat, he'll be able to nab it.

❋ Keep repeating, as he learns that it's okay to paw at the cup or even knock it over and take the treat. You want him happy and revved up for this fun game!

About Treats

Small dogs require small treats! Training treats should be about the size of a pencil eraser. If your dog has a tendency to be pudgy (and more than half of dogs are overweight), be especially careful. Give him bits of kibble (and reduce his dinner portions) rather than give him fattening treats. Cheerios and bits of carrots are treats dogs love that add almost nothing to a waistline.

❋ Once he's consistently successful at this stage, you can start moving the position of the cup with the treat (just as in the human shell game).

❋ Let him watch you place the treat under the cup, and only move the cup once at first.

❋ Tell him "Find it!"

❋ If he finds it, he gets to have the treat. Good boy!

❋ You can gradually work up to a true carnival shell game, where you put down a treat and move the cups several times.

❋ Whenever your dog gets confused with this trick (or any other), go back a step to where he was successful. Make it fun and motivating.

Some dogs pick this game up instantly, understanding exactly what you want. Others take longer to figure it out. That's okay, too. This is a game—not finding missing persons! Relax and show your dog what you want, until the "light bulb" goes on. Once your dog understands what you want, and that a treat is involved when he picks the right cup, I promise his nose will know what to do!

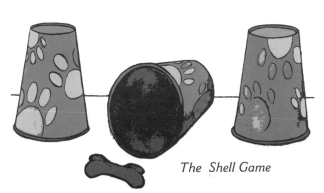

The Shell Game

Give your dog a refresher on the Come command before playing.

Game #3: Find "Bob"

To play this fabulously fun game, your dog needs to know how to come on command. If you need a refresher course on "Teaching Come" or any other command, see the Appendix.

What You'll Need

* Treats
* A friend or family member

How to Play

* You and your dog stand on one side of a room, and station a friend on the other side of the room.
* Say to your dog "Where's Bob?" (or Mary or whomever you're looking for).
* As soon as you say, "Where's Bob?" have Bob give the Come command to your dog.
* Have Bob give him a big treat for coming.
* Pause longer and longer between you saying, "Where's Bob?" and Bob's "Come" command, until your dog automatically is running to Bob when you say, "Where's Bob?"
* Bob should *always* have a treat ready when the dog "finds" him.
* After your dog has mastered "finding Bob" in plain sight, have Bob walk around a corner.

❋ Get your dog really revved up and tell him to "Find Bob!" At first, Bob can call the dog.

❋ Gradually phase out the "Come" command, so that your dog begins to look for people on your cue of the word "Find."

❋ When he finds Bob around the corner, make it a giant party! Treats! Praise! News releases to the local paper!

❋ Over time, gradually have Bob hide in more difficult places to find—and always the dog gets a major reward when he finds Bob.

Once your dog understands how to do this with one person, add other family and friends, so that your dog can find anyone in the house for you! And, of course, your family and friends can also have your dog find you.

This is a hugely interesting, rewarding game for your dog. And, if you're wondering what your teenagers are up to, your little guy is the perfect snitch!

Reward your dog when he "Finds Bob."

Game #4: Find "Goldie!"

If you have more than one dog, you might want to play this variation of "Find Bob" that I developed to help find my senior Papillon, Goldie, who happens to be deaf as a post in her old age. Goldie sleeps like a rock (nothing wakes her!), and it is often a challenge to find a tiny 6-pound (2.7 kg) dog sleeping somewhere in the house.

Luckily, I have two assistants! I just say to my Papillons, Radar and Pogo, "Where's Goldie?" They happily search from room to room until they joyfully find Goldie, snoozing away. They've now started bringing her to me, one boy on each side, nudging her rump forward with their pointy little noses! Goldie always looks just a little stunned, but she moves along as they herd her to me, as compliant as a tiny sheep. How did I teach my dogs this behavior? It was easy.

What You'll Need
❋ Another dog

How to Play
You'll need to teach your dogs each other's names. Do to this, when you give them treats, say each name and then give the treat to that dog. It teaches them to wait their turn and also has the effect of reinforcing the names of each dog to the other. Once the dogs know each other's names, then it's easy to cue on the dog's names.

❋ Start at a time when one dog is sleeping. Call the other dog to you and have him follow you.

❋ Start slowly walking from room to room whispering, "Where's Goldie?" (or the name of your sleeping dog).

❋ When you find the "lost" dog, say, "There's GOLDIE!" in a happy, thrilled voice. Praise your dog for helping out.

❋ Usually, it will take just few times of looking together before your dogs figure out how to play this "game."

When the boys find Goldie for me, and when they bring her to me, I tell them just how fabulous, wonderful, brilliant, and downright useful they are! They wag their whole bodies with pride and joy. After all, what could be more exciting, from a dog's point of view, than what they've just done? They've used their natural scenting ability to find a member of their pack, and used their natural herding abilities to bring her back to me. It's a lesson: We should never underestimate the intelligence—and the usefulness—of our little dogs.

Game #5: Hide and Seek

If your dog has a reliable Stay command, you can teach him to play "hide and seek" with you.

What You'll Need
* Treats

How to Play
* Tell your dog to "Stay" and hide just around the corner.
* Call him once—and then let him find you.
* Give him a treat and tons of praise.
* Don't hide after every Stay command—you'll just end up with a dog who follows you. Occasionally, after you've given the Stay command, return to your dog and reward him for a "Good stay!"
* Eventually you can hide in more difficult places, and give a big cheer when your dog hunts you down.

You can make a game of finding other dogs.

Game #6: Where Is It?

This game teaches your dog to find objects.

What You'll Need

❋ A toy or treat
❋ Washcloth

How to Play

❋ Take a favorite toy or a treat, and let your dog see you put it under a washcloth.
❋ Ask him, "Where is it?"
❋ When he digs and gets it, let him have the treat or play with the toy.
❋ Once he understands the game, begin to make the toy or treat just a little harder to find. Put it under your pillow, or under the bed.
❋ Over time, gradually work up to the point at which you can put the toy or treat anywhere in the room when your dog isn't looking, ask him "Where is it?" and he'll find it!
❋ Dogs can learn to find different objects if you give the objects names. So, he can learn to find his favorite ball, his stuffed bear, or other toy if you give that toy a specific name.

As your dog gets better, you can start hiding objects in more difficult places.

Game #7: Find My Keys

Once your dog knows how to find objects, he can make your life easier. For example, if you are always looking for your keys, how about teaching your dog to find them for you?

(If you like to train with a clicker, or are thinking about trying clicker training, this is a great clicker exercise. See the box on Clicker Training.)

What You'll Need

* Keys
* Treats
* Clicker (if you'd like to try clicker training)

How to Play

* Put your keys on the floor.
* Show them to your dog.
* When he reaches out with his nose to check out what you have, say, "Good keys!" (or give him a click with the clicker) and give him a reward.
* Gradually move the keys farther and farther from the dog, praising (or clicking) and treating every time he comes up and touches them.

In this exercise, it's very, very important to give big rewards—make it a party when the dog touches the keys! Remember, up until now, he's found objects that are their own reward—the people he loves, his canine buddy, his favorite toys. In those cases, the treats are just icing on an already great cake. Keys aren't interesting to a dog, and they aren't inherently rewarding. You have to provide the excitement and reward when he finds them for you, or he'll lose interest in this game.

Once your dog really gets the hang of this, and if he has a talented nose, you'll never have to worry about losing your keys again! He'll point them out to you on tables, he'll tell you they're on countertops.

By the way, the good dog who finds your keys deserves a special ride in the car to the park, don't you think?

Outdoor Scent Games: Tracking

So far, your little dog has been learning air scent games—he puts up his head, sniffs, and finds the object. Tracking or trailing is a slightly different job. A tracking dog follows the path of a person or animal. The dog sniffs the ground for clues to where the person went, rather than sniffing in the air to locate the object.

Tracking is among the most useful skills that dogs contribute to our world. When a crook runs from the scene of a crime, police dogs track the suspect's scent trail. When a person gets lost, search-and-rescue volunteers and their dogs follow the trail of the lost person. Of course, most of us never track down a criminal or have a dog who's trained enough to search for lost souls. But using your dog's tracking skills can be a whole lot of fun—time spent outside together allowing your dog to follow his fabulous nose.

You can start training a puppy as young as 3 months old in the first steps of tracking. It's a sport that dogs can enjoy well into their senior years. I was at an American Kennel Club (AKC) tracking test when a 15-year-old Border Terrier came within a whisker of passing TDX requirements (a high-ranking title in the world of tracking). That grizzled veteran was just as capable of this work as the young dogs in their prime.

For tracking, dogs wear harnesses instead of collars.

The Equipment

All you need is a harness, a long line, some treats, and a small field.

Harness

Dogs track wearing a harness instead of a collar. Because the dog leads you, and his nose is pulling you toward the scent, a dog wearing a collar would be choked. So, a comfortable harness that doesn't chafe is a necessity.

Leash and Long Line

You'll need to follow your dog at a distance, but still keep him on a leash. You can get started with a 6-foot (1.8-m) long leash. For more advanced tracking, a lightweight line of up to 40 feet (12.1 m) is needed. Retractable leashes aren't a good idea in tracking. You want to have a feel for where your dog is taking you, and the plastic handle of a retractable leash gets in the way of that communication.

Glove

At the end of the trail, you'll need a glove with treats in it. This is how your dog will know when he's made it to the end of the "trail." Traditionally, in formal AKC tracking, the glove is leather, which you can find at gardening stores. Of course, for fun, any glove will do just fine.

Treats

Not only will you need treats to put in a glove at the end of the trail, you'll also need plenty of yummy treats to put along the track. Think about the location of your track when you decide which treats to use. In the beginning, you lay a short track that the dog will quickly follow as he eat the treats, so almost any yummy treat will do. However, as you practice, you will "age" the tracks, or allow them to stand for a while before your dog follows them. You'll

---

Finding and Fitting a Harness

Look for a harness that is made of soft materials. Leather harnesses should be buttery soft, or use a nylon or cotton harness instead. In tracking, the dog pulls you forward, so his harness must fit comfortably. Make sure it's secure and comfortable across the front of your dog's chest, and not fitted overly tight around his rib cage. Look for a harness that allows you to adjust it, so you can make sure the fit is just right.

Tracking is a fun sport for many dogs.

find then that other creatures are interested in the treats, too. (I was once practicing tracking with Radar and realized that birds were happily snacking on all the treats I'd laid out for him!) If you're tracking in summer, use a treat that doesn't draw ants or other pests. One favorite among trackers is dehydrated lamb lung pieces—they're delicious to dogs and don't seem to attract bugs.

Field

Although you can attempt to lay a track in your backyard, keep in mind your scent is already criss-crossed all over your yard, making it difficult for your dog to follow a particular track. If you decide to use your backyard, keep the track short and use tempting treats. A quiet yard or field that doesn't have a lot of scents is ideal for tracking. A park can be a good place, but not one where lots of kids are creating their own scent trails. Farmers' fields are ideal (with permission, of course). Your dog is *always* on a leash, so the field doesn't need secure fencing. When you start tracking, you'll lay a track only a few feet long, so you don't have to find great acreage! (Experienced dogs will enjoy working large areas, though.)

Laying a Track

* Pick the area to lay your track (preferably in short grass, and away from a lot of foot traffic, which could confuse the scent).
* If it's windy, walk into it (so it doesn't blow the scent away).
* Put your dog in a harness and have someone hold him (or tie him securely

where he can watch you).

* Put one foot down, and place a treat right at your toe.

* Take a *small* step, and put a treat right at the toe of your other foot.

* Take a total of 10 "baby steps," leaving a treat at the toe of your footprint. (Think of your footprint as being an arrow for the dog, pointing right to the treat.)

* At the end of the track, put down your glove with a yummy stash of treats. This is the jackpot for finding the end of your trail, so be generous!

* Put the dog at the beginning of the track, and give your command (a word such as "Find!").

* If he doesn't see the treats, point them out to him.

* Once he puts his nose down, just follow along, until he comes to the glove.

* When he finds the glove, show him the yummy treats inside, then praise and play! Yes! He's a hero dog!

* Once he gets the idea, slowly make the track a little longer. Start spacing the treats two and then three steps apart.

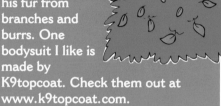

What About Those Prickly Bushes?

Many little dogs have long, easily matted fur. If you will be out in the fields practicing your tracking, consider getting a Lycra bodysuit to cover your dog from head to toe, to protect his fur from branches and burrs. One bodysuit I like is made by K9topcoat. Check them out at www.k9topcoat.com.

Doggy goggles can protect your dog's eyes.

Once your little guy has had some practice, you can add turns.

❋ Walk about 20 feet (6 m), make a 90-degree turn, putting a treat at each toe for the first three steps after the turn.

❋ As always, at the end of the track lies the glove with the treats.

❋ Start with a track that has one right turn, and then add two right turns, and then three.

Then lay a track with one left turn, and then two left turns, and then three.

Not everyone wants to become a serious tracker. Even if you just do a straight track for several feet on occasion, it will teach your dog the fun and adventure of hanging out with you. It will teach him to offer new behaviors, and it will increase his confidence. You just might become hooked on a great sport. If you and your dog love being outside in the fresh air together, and you feel bonded together in this most primal of dog activities, pursue it.

Whether you become a serious hobbyist or just play some tracking games with your dog, try this sport. It will bring out a part of your little dog that might forever remain dormant if you don't.

The tracks can get more difficult as your dog gets the hang of it.

Important Job

When you think of law-enforcement dogs, you probably think of German Shepherd Dogs patrolling with police departments around the country. Well, some little dogs are part of the national defense, too.

The Beagle Brigade works as part of the U.S. Department of Agriculture (USDA) Animal and Plant Health Inspection Service. They're on duty at airports throughout the country, sniffing out illegal foods brought into the United States. The Beagles wear green jackets with "Protecting American Agriculture" on one side and "Agriculture's Beagle Brigade" on the other.

The dogs are trained to sniff up to 50 different odors, including citrus fruit, mango, apple, beef, or pork. Beagles are lovers, not fighters: When they sniff the banned substances, they sit quietly. The Beagle Brigade nabs about 75,000 prohibited agricultural products a year. The dogs are given a food reward when they find a suspicious odor. An experienced Beagle successfully sniffs out the contraband about 90 percent of the time.

Although this job may not seem as exotic as sniffing for drugs or bombs, it's very important. Insect infestations and plant disease can be introduced through contraband foods, so these dogs help keep agriculture safe in the United States.

Using Scent Skills in Service to Others

Mostly, scent games for little dogs are just fun. But if you find you absolutely love to do these nose games, and you have a high-energy little dog who needs a job, your dog's nose could save a life.

Volunteer Search-and-Rescue Teams

Highly trained dogs volunteer as search-and-rescue dogs. They look for lost hikers, find people with Alzheimer's disease who have strayed from home, and even help in times of national disaster. While most of these dogs are large working breeds, such as German Shepherd Dogs and Labrador Retrievers, a real need exists for smaller dogs, too. Small dogs are the best candidates to check for survivors in a pile of rubble, or to worm through a small tunnel in search of a lost child.

These dogs typically have 2 or 3 years of training before they're ready to go on an assignment. This is all-volunteer work, so there's no payment—except

Flat-Faced Breeds: Consider Doggles

Short-nosed breeds such as Pugs and English Toy Spaniels can learn to track. However, their eyes are at some risk as they sniff their way through the grass. Part of the problem is that their eyes protrude almost as much as their noses, so it's easy for a stray blade of grass or even a stick to come in contact with their eyes.

But the problem is even worse for the smush-faced breeds. The changes in their facial structure caused by their flattened noses decreases the nerve transmission from their eyes to their brains. As a result, many (although certainly not all) flat-nosed dogs don't experience pain in their eyes. They won't blink when an object comes near their eyes, and they don't show signs of pain when their eyes have been injured.

A good solution is to get protective eyewear for your flat-faced dog. The most well-known brand of doggy goggles is Doggles. Check them out at www.doggles.com.

for the satisfaction you'll get from important work done well. Small dogs *can* do this work: I have an acquaintance whose Jack Russell Terrier is a search-and-rescue dog.

If this idea sings to your heart, check out the National Association for Search & Rescue at www.nasar.org, and click on "Specialty Fields" for information about search and rescue using dogs.

Dogs can use their noses to help others.

Finding Lost Pets

When a human is lost, teams of people look to safely bring that person home. When a dog or cat is lost, almost no resources are available. Kathy "Kat" Albrecht wants to change that. She's a former canine cop who has started training programs for people to become real-life pet detectives.

The US Department of Agriculture uses Beagles to help sniff out illegal foodstuffs.

For information about how you and your dog can find training in this field, check out Pet Hunters International, www.pethunters.com. Who knows? You and your dog might just find a new career.

Even if you have no desire to change jobs, you'll enjoy Albrecht's fascinating book, *The Lost Pet Chronicles: Adventures of a K-9 Cop Turned Pet Detective.*

You never know where your dog's nose will lead you. The only way to find out is to start by playing some games. So, put a treat in your hand, and ask your dog: "Which hand?"

Turn Your Living Room into Disneyland for Dogs:

Chapter 3

Agility, Flyball, and Dancing

There isn't a dog in the world excited over you asking, "Hey boy, you wanna watch TV??!! Huh?! Huh?! Let's watch some TV!" But that's how most small dogs spend their free time—watching TV with their people. (You'd think with such a large dog demographic, the cable shows would come with closed-captioned barking.)

It doesn't have to be this way. You can turn your house into a playground for your pup. The great thing about having a small dog is that they don't require a lot of room. You don't need a farm—you don't even need a backyard—for him to get plenty of exercise.

This chapter will teach you the delights of playing "Living Room Agility"—a fast-paced and rousing good time for all. And while you're jumping and running, how about creating a Flyball course in your home? Then, for those tender moments, it's time to put on "your song" and dance, dance, dance!

Living Room Agility

You've probably heard of agility—it's become the world's most popular dog sport. Dogs run an obstacle course, flying over hurdles, caroming through above-ground tunnels, snaking through weave poles, and tip-toeing over dog walks that are the canine equivalent of a gymnast's balance beam.

You can turn your living room into an agility course. All you'll need is some foam board, a few (unused!) toilet board, a few (unused!) toilet

Agility is a fast-paced fun sport for dogs.

plunges, one or two kid's tunnels from a toy store, a towel, and two footstools. Don't worry, all this "equipment" picks up in minutes and stores quickly and easily into small spaces.

Admittedly, Living Room Agility isn't regulation agility, but it will give you a fun taste of the sport, and it's a great bonding experience for your little guy. It's a bit like playing a game of basketball in the driveway, while the agility you see on *Animal Planet* is more akin to an NBA game. Still, it's a fun time that helps you keep your dog fit and builds basic agility skills—just as a child playing hoops in the driveway could be the start of a sports career.

Supplies

As I mentioned, the supplies for Living Room Agility are easily found. Here's what you'll need:

* **For the hurdles:** foam board
* **For the tunnels:** a kid's tunnel (if you have room, buy 2) and a towel
* **For the weave poles:** toilet plungers
* **For the dogwalk:** your couch and 2 footstools

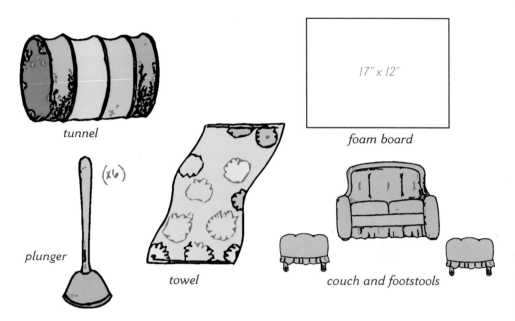

tunnel

foam board

17" x 12"

(x6)

plunger

towel

couch and footstools

Supplies for a living room agility course.

Hurdles

The sport of agility grew out of entertainment at horse shows, where the athletic dogs jumped over the horse's jumps between the equine competitive rounds. Hurdles are still the heart of agility, so your Living Room Agility course should include them.

Caution: Agility Can Cause Injuries!

Agility is one of the few dog sports that can cause serious injury. The exercises in this book are for fun only and don't include regulation equipment like A-frames and dogwalks that pose the most danger for your dog. Still, these tasks are asking your dog to run and jump—and potential danger always exists in those activities, even for a young and healthy dog.

If your dog has any physical problem, such as arthritis or luxating patellas, this style of play could make his condition worse. If he has limited eyesight, jumping is downright dangerous. Some dogs with disabilities can and do enjoy agility, but *always, always, always talk with your veterinarian* before asking any dog to do agility—even Living Room Agility!

How to Make Portable Hurdles

The hurdles for Living Room Agility don't need to stand up to the wear and tear of major competition. You can make yours out of lightweight foam board from a craft store. These hurdles cost just pennies. It's so easy, even I can do it. (And anyone who knows me understands I'm not exactly the Princess of Do-It-Yourself.)

The hurdles use only two components: braces and a main board.

Braces

❋ Cut two strips of foam board, about 12 inches (30 cm) long and 2 inches (5 cm) high.

❋ Cut a 1-inch (2.5-cm) notch into the top of the strips, at the center.

Main Board

❋ Cut another strip as wide as the foam board will allow. (If you want a wider hurdle, tape two pieces of foam board together.)

❋ Cut the board 1-inch (2.5-cm) less than the height you want your dog to

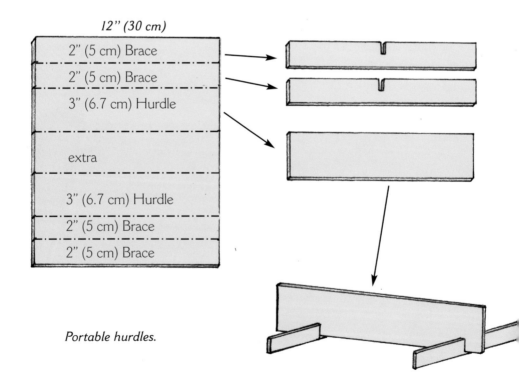

Portable hurdles.

jump. (For example, if your dog is jumping 4 inches (10 cm), cut a 3-inch (6.7 cm) strip.)

To assemble, stick the main board into the notches of the braces—you have a jump that is sturdy enough for indoor use. Foam board will blow over (or away!) in windy conditions, so this is an indoor-only device.

How High?

The point of agility isn't to see how high a dog can jump. Instead, determining stride and timing the jump are what make jumping interesting for a dog. It's like a canine geometry problem, done at high speed. So for them, it's just as much fun to jump 2 inches (5 cm) as it is to jump 12 or 22 inches (30 or 56 cm). So, to decrease the chances of injury, keep your jumps low. Two inches (5 cm) is fine for little dogs. Don't ever ask the dog to jump higher than his height at the top of his shoulders (the withers).

Dogs need enough room to approach a hurdle and jump it. The lower the hurdle, the less room they need. So, if you have a small room, it's important to have low hurdles. When you're doing several hurdles in a row, always keep at least 8 feet (2.4 m) between the hurdles, so the dog has time to gather himself between jumps.

Jumping Is NOT for Dogs Under a Year Old!

Never, ever give your dog a "Jump" command until he is fully and completely grown. For most toy dogs, this is usually at about a year old.

Why? Puppies have growth plates, where the bones on their legs join. If those joints are stressed, you could cause your little guy serious injury and life-time pain.

You may see your puppy naturally jumping on his own, but that is different from giving him a "Jump" command. A puppy won't jump on his own if he's uncomfortable. However, a puppy wants to follow what you say to please you—and he'll jump even when it hurts.

Puppies have bumps on their front legs that show they are still growing. If your puppy still has these bumps, do not *ever* give him a Jump command. Once the bumps are gone, and he's over a year old, it's time to ask your veterinarian if it's okay to ask your dog to jump.

Teaching the Hurdles

Your dog has four excellent little feet, and he already knows how to jump, right?

Well, not exactly. Remember, you want your dog to jump where and when you ask—after all, it's a team sport. You're the coach with your dog. So, if he jumps sort of randomly, the game won't be as much fun for either of you.

Also, you want to make sure that, even in Living Room Agility, your dog is learning to jump safely. This might be the foundation for a whole new activity for you both. The better, safer form he has at the beginning, the less chance of injury he'll have later.

To teach a dog to jump on command:

❋ Place the hurdles in such a way that your dog will have no choice but to go over. A great place to put hurdles is a hallway, with one side touching a wall.

❋ Walk beside your dog down the hallway, placing him so that, when he comes to the hurdle, he is almost automatically going to jump it.

❋ Start about 8 feet (2.4 m) away from the jump.

❋ Don't put the dog on a leash—you want him to be free to navigate the jump on his own. Move quickly enough so that he feels the sense of excitement.

❋ When you get near your 2-inch (5-cm) high jump, say "Over" (or "Jump" or whatever command you choose).

❋ You can jump over the little jump with your dog, so he sees how much fun it is.

❋ After he's jumped, tell him he's great! He's terrific! He's a mini Michael Jordan!

After you've practiced jumping together, he can start to practice jumping alone.

Always Warm Up Before Jumping

Even with little jumps, it's important to warm your dog's muscles up before jumping to prevent muscle sprains, strains, and other problems. Let him run around on the ground, do Come commands, or have him run alongside you. Once he's warmed up for a few minutes, you can begin jumping.

❋ Step farther and farther away from the hurdle. Eventually, you can have him stay at one side of the hurdle, then call him to you with the Over command.

❋ You can give him a treat for a job well done, but part of the reward for jumping is the sheer joy of the exercise itself for a dog.
Most dogs catch on right away.

If Your Dog Doesn't Jump

If your dog is reluctant to jump, some possible reasons include:

❋ He may be afraid you're going to step on him, especially if the jump area is crowded. Make sure he has enough room, and that you're walking in a straight line. If you're veering in toward the dog, it will make him hold back.

❋ If he still doesn't like running with you, try another way of teaching jumping. Have someone hold the dog (about 8 feet [2.4 m] from the hurdle). Stand a few steps behind the hurdle, holding a treat. Show him the treat and call him. When he gathers himself to jump, say "Over" so that he begins to associate the command with jumping.

❋ The hurdle may be too high. If you have a little dog, start the jumping at 2 inches (5 cm). An 8-inch high (20-cm) jump looks like a wall to a tiny Yorkie or Chihuahua—they must learn to build up to those heights. (The concept of a "high jump" is relative.)

❋ The floor may be too slick. Dogs don't want to jump from or land on slippery surfaces. Do this activity on carpet.

❋ It's possible that he has a physical problem that makes jumping uncomfortable. Put aside the jumps for now and watch him. Does he normally comfortably jump on the couch, the bed, and other objects? Or does he ask for a boost up? Back problems can happen in any breed, and these are especially common in long-

Always Supervise Jumping

For safety's sake, put the jumps away when you aren't there to supervise the jumping. Because the foam board jumps are lightweight and come apart easily, they're easy to disassemble and can store in any closet.

backed breeds such as Dachshunds and Corgis. It never hurts to have your vet check a dog who's reluctant to jump.

Remember, Living Room Agility is just one activity in this book. If it doesn't suit your dog, there's plenty of others that will be perfect for him.

Once your dog is a proficient jumper, you can have fun with the jumps. Construct several hurdles and put them up around the house when you want to play. Together, race around the house, with him jumping over the hurdles and having fun. You can always double-back, so even a small apartment with only two or three jumps can provide a lot excitement.

Tunnels, Tunnels, Tunnels

Tunnels are one of the most interesting obstacles in agility. Two types of agility tunnels are used: open and collapsed. You can have a mini-version of each in your Living Room course.

The Open Tunnel

In regulation competition, the open tunnel is a large, portable fixture that has a bend in the middle. They're big and heavy. For practice with your pint-sized companion, a child's tunnel works perfectly. They're about 4 to 8 feet (1.2 to 2.4 m) long, widely available at toy stores, and relatively inexpensive. Some brands are made so that you can attach several tunnels together, which is a great idea if you're later practicing for competition. For play, a single kid's tunnel is more than enough.

Teaching the Open Tunnel

* Start with the tunnel folded like an accordion (about a foot [.3 m] long). Different tunnels fold slightly differently. The idea is to try to make the

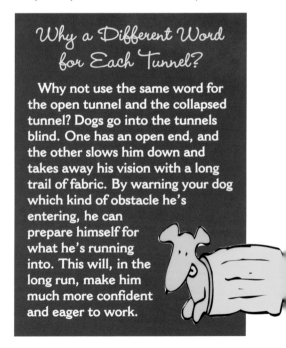

Why a Different Word for Each Tunnel?

Why not use the same word for the open tunnel and the collapsed tunnel? Dogs go into the tunnels blind. One has an open end, and the other slows him down and takes away his vision with a long trail of fabric. By warning your dog which kind of obstacle he's entering, he can prepare himself for what he's running into. This will, in the long run, make him much more confident and eager to work.

tunnel fold in such a way that your dog has a surface that feels safe to walk on (not too many bumps or wrinkles).

❋ If you can't make the surface comfortable for the dog, unfold the tunnel so that the surface is smooth. See the section below, "If Your Dog Doesn't Want to Tunnel" for instructions on how to teach the Tunnel command if you have to unfold the tunnel right away.

Example of an open tunnel.

❋ Have a friend hold your dog at one end of the tunnel (or put him on a Stay command if he has a reliable stay) while you stand at the other end of the tunnel. (For a refresher course on the Stay command, check out the Appendix.)

❋ Show him a yummy, delicious, tempting treat.

❋ Hold the treat inside the tunnel and call him to you.

❋ After you call him, have your friend let your dog go.

❋ Give him the treat as he enters the tunnel.

❋ Repeat, giving him the treat a little farther into the tunnel each time.

❋ Continue to reward later and later, until you can hold the treat outside the exit of the folded tunnel, and he happily runs to get it.

❋ Now, it's time to add the command word "Tunnel." Hold the treat outside the folded tunnel and, as he barrels toward it, say "Tunnel! Good!"

❋ Once he understands the basic concept, you can begin unfolding the tunnel, making it longer and longer.

❋ He gets the reward when he successfully navigates through the contraption.

If Your Dog Doesn't Want to Tunnel

❋ Your little dog may not take to the tunnel right away. Here's what may be causing it, and what to do:

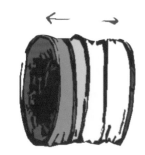

* He may not like the surface of the folded tunnel on his feet. It's scary for a dog to walk on an uneven, folded surface, and that can be a problem. Try unfolding the tunnel just enough to give him a safe-feeling place to put his feet. If you need to, unfold the entire length of the tunnel.

Keep the tunnel folded at first.

* You may be going a bit fast for him. Try slowing it down:
  1. Sit with your dog at the mouth of the tunnel.
  2. Feed him his favorite treat.
  3. Then hold the favorite treat inside the tunnel, so he has to put his head in the tunnel to get the treat.
  4. Then hold the treat farther in, so his front paws also are in the tunnel.
  5. Eventually, treat him to his absolutely favorite snack while he's standing in the tunnel.
  6. Then have your friend hold the dog (or put the dog in a stay) while you go to the other end of the tunnel.
  7. Toss a bit of his favorite treat into the tunnel, aiming close to the opening next to your dog.
  8. When he ventures in for the treat, praise him!
  9. Gradually, toss the treats farther along the tunnel, so he has to venture farther and farther in.
  10. Laugh! Clap! Tell him he's such a cool dog!

* Teach by example—yes, that means that you're going to go into the tunnel! Have your dog at one end of the tunnel, while you come through the other, ending up face-to-face with the dog. Show him that you think the tunnel is a happy, safe, fun place to be. Merrily lure him with his favorite treat while you are inside, reminding him

Use a towel to replicate a collapsed tunnel.

that he's the coolest tunnel rat on the planet. Gradually, have him come farther and farther into the tunnel. If he's worried, don't rush him too fast. Don't put a lot of pressure on him. Just have fun.

* If he seems worried, you can leave the tunnel out and put treats and toys inside,

Example of a collapsed tunnel.

so he can explore it at his own pace over time. He'll eventually decide it's fun to get the treats in the tunnel—and then you have it made.

Tunnels are a very safe piece of equipment. The kids' tunnels fold up well, and they're lightweight and easy to store. It's also okay to leave the tunnels out (unlike jumps) for the dog to play in. If you have a cat, expect your feline to love to play in the tunnel, too!

Collapsed Tunnels

The collapsed tunnel is also found in regulation agility. It's a short tunnel with a long expanse of cloth draped over the end. To replicate a collapsed tunnel in your living room, attach a towel to the end of a kid's tunnel.

Teaching the Collapsed Tunnel

* Start practicing this equipment after your dog has mastered the regular tunnel and merrily goes through an open tunnel on command.
* Gather the towel at the top of the tunnel, and give your dog his "Tunnel" command.
* Reward him when he comes through.
* Lower the towel a little, so he sees the fabric, but it's still too high to touch him.
* Give the Tunnel command, but also add the word "Chute" (or whatever word you'd like to use for the collapsed tunnel). So, you'll be saying, "Ready?! Ready?! Tunnel! Good chute!" Anytime he's in a situation where

he might be able to see the fabric—and certainly if he's going to be touching the fabric—use the word "Chute" to warn him that this is the tunnel that has the "wall" he has to run through.

* Over time, gradually let the towel drape farther and farther down the opening of the tunnel, until it eventually covers the opening and the bottom lies on the ground.

Get your dog used to having things touch his head.

If Your Dog Doesn't Want to Go Through the Collapsed Tunnel

* Slow down. You've probably gone too fast. Make sure he understands the "Tunnel" command on the open tunnel. Then go back to square one, and

Hold up the end of the collapsed tunnel at first.

introduce the fabric drape at a glacial pace.

* He may not like things in his face. Check to see if he has any eye or teeth problems that could make him want to shy away from things touching his face. Most dogs aren't used to things touching their faces, and they prefer not to have their faces bothered. Help solve this problem by touching your dog's face a lot.

* When you touch your dog's face, give him treats and tell him he's wonderful. I like to teach my dogs the names of all their body parts: ears, nose, teeth, eyes (and also the rest of the body, feet, tail, tummy, etc.). Over time, he'll associate being touched—even on his face—with a happy time. He'll realize the collapsing tunnel is one more fun experience that just happens to involve something touching his face.

Don't Want to Spring for a Tunnel?

If you don't want to spend the money on a kid's tunnel, use a cardboard box (or a couple of cardboard boxes taped together). Your dog doesn't care about looks. He just wants to play! If you have kids, they might even have fun decorating the boxes for the Living Room Agility Course.

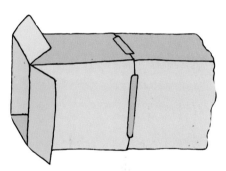

You can make your own tunnel out of boxes.

The Couch "Dogwalk"

Agility equipment is unwieldy and takes up a lot of room. Only a dedicated participant would tolerate all that equipment in her home (A-frames and elevated dogwalks take up more space than the average person's family room!).

For Living Room Agility, you can use your couch instead. But exercise some caution. On real agility obstacles, a yellow "contact zone" is placed at the bottom of the obstacle. The dogs much touch this zone before attempting the obstacle, so they won't leap down and put strain on their joints. Even for athletic little dogs playing Living Room Agility, it's not a good idea to command them to jump on and (especially!) off a couch at high speeds.

You can make your own "contact zones" by putting footstools at each end of

Contact Zone   Contact Zone

Use your couch as a "dogwalk."

the couch. Your dog will be required to jump on the footstool, pause a second for a treat, run across the couch, jump down to the other footstool, collect another treat, and run through the rest of the course.

Teaching the Couch Dogwalk

Start by running with your dog, showing him what you want. Give every piece of equipment a name.

* For the first obstacle—jumping on the footstool—say "Up the Stool," hold the treat at the footstool, and give the treat when your dog jumps on the footstool.

* For the second obstacle, running along the cushions, say "Up Couch!" and run along the couch with him. The best choice is for the dog to go along the seat of the couch, not across the back, because you don't want him falling off and injuring himself. Run with him—tell him he's great. (You LOVE dogs on the furniture!)

* At the end of the couch, direct him to a footstool at the end of the couch, with an "Off Stool" command. Again, reward the dog for stopping, so that he learns to control the jump and takes it slowly and carefully.

When you run with your dog along the Couch Obstacle, cheer, clap, and always reward the pauses on the "contact" footstools!

Use plungers to make your own weave poles.

Weave Poles

There's a secret some agility competitors may not want out there, but I'm here to reveal it: They practice weave poles in their homes—using toilet plungers! You can do the same for your Living Room Agility course. All you'll need is 6 new plungers (don't even think about the look you'll get at the checkout stand from the cashier).

Weave poles are a difficult obstacle, and long treatises have been written about the best way to teach a dog weave poles. Here, we'll just do some fun basic weaving. If you're interested in trying competition agility, all kinds of gadgets, gizmos, and approaches are available to make your dog weave faster

Weave poles are a difficult obstacle in agility.

Sample living room agility course.

and more nimbly. But let's face it: You're only going to get up to a certain speed in the house anyway, so there's no need to get too carried away. The idea is to train your dog to run as straight as possible without hitting the poles, much like a slalom skier does in the Olympics.

Teaching Weave Poles

* Set the plungers in a straight line, spacing them about 20 inches (50.8 cm) apart from each other. (This is a great hallway exercise.)
* Dogs always enter the weave poles with the first pole on their left side, then slalom through them.
* Because the toilet plunger weave poles aren't tall, you can easily lure your dog along with a favorite treat or toy.
* Train one pole at a time: Use the command "Weave!," then reward; "Weave!" and reward, until you are through all the plungers.

Running the Course

You've done it: You've got an agility course in your home! You've got hurdles spaced around the living room, the couch dogwalk, the open and collapsing tunnel—and even weave poles. You and your dog will have a great time playing on the course together.

All the equipment quickly stows out of the way in case the neighbors are coming over. And, if they're great neighbors, they might come over to play agility with their dog, too!

Hallway Flyball

Flyball is a sort of "extreme sport" for dogs. It is a relay race between two teams made up of four dogs on each team. Two courses are set up side-by-side, with four hurdles on each. At the end of each set of hurdles is a spring-loaded box with balls inside. The first dog on each team flies over the hurdles, smacks the box with his paws, catches the ball that spits out of the box, then flies back over the hurdles with the ball in his mouth. As soon as the first dog on the team clears the last hurdle, the second member of the team is off and running for his turn.

At Flyball tournaments, the action is more like a car race than anything else. Flashing lights signal the starts, and electronic timing devices are used to determine the winners by a thousandth of a second. This is a noisy sport, because dogs are barking with all the excitement, and it's big-time fun for fleet-footed canine athletes!

You may not be able to match the theatrics of competitive Flyball, but you can play your own version of this game in your hallway.

Supplies
* For the hurdles: foam board
* Ball: tennis ball or ball of appropriate size for your dog's mouth

Teaching Hallway Flyball
* Play fetch with your dog using a tennis ball or other size-appropriate ball. You must teach your dog to really, really want to retrieve a tennis ball. Have fun! Make your dog love to retrieve that ball! The more the dog loves to play with his tennis ball (of whatever size), the more he will love Flyball.
* Once your dog responds to playing fetch, add hurdles.
* Review the section on hurdles in Living Room Agility. You want your dog to be experienced at jumping over the hurdles on command—if you have an energetic, bored little dog, this won't take long.
* Place the hurdles (up to four) at least 8 feet (2.4 m) apart from each other.
* Combine the hurdles and the retrieve by throwing the ball over a hurdle and telling your dog to "Get it!"
* When he grabs the ball, call him back, and give him praise,

Little Balls for Little Dogs

If you have a little dog whose mouth is tinier than a tennis ball, don't worry. Pet supply stores stock little version of tennis balls that even a Chihuahua or Yorkie can easily carry.

If you need some tips on helping your dog develop a reliable "Fetch" for Flyball, check out Chapter 4.

Flyball Boxes

A Flyball box is a spring-loaded device that pops a ball into the air when the dog hits it with his paw. These devices are expensive, and many casual players won't want to make the investment. However, Flyball boxes can be a great way to keep a high-energy dog occupied. I have a friend who bought a Flyball box for her Border Collie to keep him amused. The dog smacks the box, the ball goes flying, and he chases it. He can play a game of fetch by himself, sort of like a tennis player hitting a ball against a wall. If your dog is having a lot of fun with the chase aspects of this sport, it might be a great dog toy to invest in.

treats, and a party for doing such a grand and wonderful thing!

* Later, have a friend or spouse hold the ball at the end of the course. Toss the ball for the dog to nab in mid-air, and have him come running back.

* If you have two or more dogs, let them be their own little relay team.

* Of course, Hallway Flyball can't quite match the fun and excitement of the real deal. To learn more about the sport, upcoming tournaments, and the location of a Flyball club near you, go to the North American Flyball Association at www.flyball.org.

Canine Musical Freestyle—Do You Love Me...Now That I Can Dance?

Okay, you can admit it: You've been dancing with your dog in the privacy of your own home for years. Who hasn't? Now you can combine your love of music and your love for your dog with Canine Musical Freestyle (also known as "Dancing with Dogs"). It's the perfect activity to practice in your living room, and now that it's an official sport, it's suddenly not only socially acceptable—it's hip. What could be better?

How It Works

Musical freestylers choreograph a routine with their dog to fit with music. Basically, the routine is a process of heeling creatively, and then incorporating a lot of tricks—all in time with the rhythm of the song. Experienced freestylers have dramatic routines with fabulous costumes (and the dogs get to wear costumes, too).

Dancing with Dogs is becoming a popular activity.

Selecting a Song

This sport highlights the emotions we share with our dogs. You should pick a song that reflects who your dog is, and what your relationship together means. It's a great sport for dogs who are older or disabled, because you'll tailor the tricks to what your dog is physically capable of doing. So, if your dog can't jump well, you don't have to jump. If he moves slowly, you can pick a slow, sweet song like, "You Are So Beautiful." On the other hand, if you've got a fast, flashy dog, you can leap together to salsa music, and perform any type of fun tricks that your dog can handle.

The trick to finding a song that makes this sport truly look like dancing is to find music that reflects the rhythm of your dog's natural movement. Play a lot of music, and see what fits him. (If you're getting serious about dancing, you'll want to videotape your dog's movement, then play music to find the style that matches the timing of his gait.)

Creating a Routine

Once you've picked the music, spend time listening to it. Every song has natural segments, where rhythms change and then flow at a different pace. Chart those beats, and think about what movements fit in those timeframes. (See "Ten Basic Freestyle Moves" for typical moves to choreograph.)

Once you've decided on your moves, think about the *transitions* from one move to the next. If you

Costumes help bring a dance routine together.

58

want to go from weaves (your dog threads between your legs) to a back-up (you back away from each other), you need to design steps that put you face-to-face. That's part of the fun and artistry of this sport.

Costumes

To top it all off, at competitions, both dogs and people are in costume. Sometimes, the people costumes are quite elaborate, but dog costumes tend to be simpler. The dog's costume can't inhibit his movement, so it's generally some kind of decorative neckwear and possibly wristbands.

Ten Basic Freestyle Moves

Canine Freestyle is composed basically of tricks set to music, and you can use any tricks you like. There are no limitations and no requirements. In fact, creativity is encouraged! The most commonly used moves are described here. Also take a look at Chapter 5 for more tricks to incorporate into your routine.

Heel

Heel is the basic building block of a freestyle routine. Heeling means that you and your dog are moving as a team. In canine freestyle, you're moving as a team to music. The more precisely your dog heels, the better you will look!

Here's how to teach a small dog to heel. (The basic Heel position always has your dog walking precisely along your left side.)

* Determine a target point on your shin that is level with your dog's nose. (You don't want him looking up—which is bad for his back—or down.)

* Hold a treat at the target point.

* When your dog focuses on the target point say, "Good heel!" and give him the treat. (Some people use a stick or even a wooden spoon with a treat that the dog can target. If you do this, make sure you keep the target stick at an absolutely consistent place, or your dog won't know what to do or where to look when you fade the target stick away.)

* Once he's consistently focusing on the target spot when you say "Heel!" give him the command "Heel" and take a small step.

* Reward him with a treat as he moves with you. (Tip: Use easily chewed treats so that he doesn't stop and chew!)

* Start with a single step, then two.

* Build up distance very gradually over time.

To Learn More About Canine Freestyle

To find out more about this up-and-coming sport (and doing it outside the confines of your living room), go to the World Canine Freestyle Organization, www.worldcaninefreestyle.org.

Heel Right

This is the same as heeling, but on your right side. A good freestyle routine is balanced, and the ability to heel on both sides can be part of that balance. Of course, your dog will need a different command word, such as "Right" or "Side." Follow the same directions as for the left-sided Heel, but teach this exercise separately, so that your dog doesn't get confused.

Front

Freestyle is fluid, and you'll often want your dog in front of you, instead of at your side. You must teach him to stand directly and squarely in front of you.

* Call your dog to come.

* When he's about halfway to you, bend over—keeping your knees straight—holding a treat in front of your legs. (Yes—bending is always part of the act for small-dog trainers!)

* Hold the treat at your dog's nose level.

* When he stands squarely in front of you, give him the treat. Add a

command word, such as "Front."

* Over time, straighten up, and use the treat as a reward for being in perfect position in front of you.
* Phase out the "Come" part of this exercise—front should mean to stand squarely in front of you from wherever the dog starts.

Weave

In the weave, your dog weaves through your legs, gliding between your legs with each step you take. This is one of those exercises that make you glad you have a little dog! It's sometimes astonishing watching a big dog trying to thread through the legs of a short woman. It's a lot cuter when a little dog zips through our ankles!

* Stand with your feet about 12 inches (.3 m) apart.
* Hold a treat at knee height and lure your dog between your legs.
* When he follows the treat, tell him "Good weave!"
* At first, stand still and just reward for one pass between your legs. Then, ask him to pass between your legs, take a second step, and ask him to weave again—and then give him a big reward! Over time, work up to a

Hand Signals

A freestyle routine is flashiest when you can't hear the dog receiving commands. It truly seems like dog and human are just dancing together. The trick is to use hand signals to let the dog know what you want him to do.

Hand signals are easy to teach your dog, and they help keep him focused on you. Dogs naturally read body language, because they use their bodies to communicate. Most dog will notice your hand movements and respond quickly.

You can invent a hand signal for any exercise. It's easiest for the dog to learn a signal when it's an extension of the way you held the treat to lure the dog into the exercise in the first place. So, in doggie dancing, you teach a "weave" by luring the dog through your legs with a treat. The signal for your weaves can eventually be dipping your hands down at your sides—the beginning of that luring motion. To people, you'll look a little like John Travolta. To your dog, you'll look a little like a Pez dispenser!

pass with several weaves before giving him the treat.

Twist

In this exercise, the dog twirls in a counterclockwise direction. It's the canine equivalent of a pirouette, and it is used often in freestyle. It's flashy and it's easy to teach.

* With the dog in the Front position, hold a treat in your *left* hand.
* Take a step back with your *left* foot to encourage your dog to move, and lure the dog with the treat to your left side. Hold the treat at his nose level, luring him into a counterclockwise turn. Once he understands what you're asking, give the command a name, such as "Twist!"
* He will do an about turn on your left side, and come back into the heel position.
* Reward him when he comes back to the heel position.
* As your dog begins to understand "Twist," stop moving your left leg: You stand still, and your dog does the moving.
* Once he understands the movement you want, start having him "twist" in all sorts of different positions, not just at your side. (Experienced freestylers have dogs twisting across the stage from them!)

Teach your dog some basic obedience commands before you start dancing.

Spin

Spin is the same motion as Twist, but done in a clockwise direction. Follow the directions for "Twist," but hold the treat in your right hand. Some dogs turn much better in one direction than another, so find out if spins or twists are easier for your dog, and think about that as you incorporate them into a routine.

Circle

This command has the dog trotting in a circle around you while you stand still.

❀ With your dog in the Front position, hold a treat in your right hand.

❀ Take a step back with your right leg to get the dog moving.

❀ Hold the treat in front of the dog and lure him around the back of your legs to your left side. (Okay—this can feel a little awkward. Eventually, you'll be standing still, facing forward while your dog circles you, so come as close to that position as you can while you're holding a treat in front of his nose.)

❀ Give him the treat when he's sitting at your left side. Tell him, "Good circle!"

❀ When your dog begins to understand the exercise, stop moving your right leg.

There are variations you can train on Circle (using different words for your dog with each variation). For example, you can teach your dog to only circle your left or right leg—something of a cross between Circle and Weave.

Back-Up

One of the flashier moves in freestyle is when the dog and handler back away from each other, farther and farther, to the beat of the music.

❀ With your dog in the Front position, take a tiny, little, nonthreatening step toward him.

❀ The moment he backs up just a tiny bit, tell him "Good Back!" and reward him.

❀ Gradually phase in more and more steps in his back-up command.

Advanced freestylers and their dogs dance back from each other for several feet at a time.

You can combine Back-Up with heeling, creating a Heel Back move. Once your dog understands the concept of walking backward on his own, he can learn to heel backward with you. When I heel backward with Radar, I say "Heel back," combing his Heel command and his Back command. He understands this combination, and can now heel backward very effectively.

Reverse Circle

This is an extension of the Heel Back move.

* With your dog at your left side, circle backward. At first, both you and your dog will circle together. Be very enthusiastic, telling your dog he's brilliant! Label this move (Radar's word is "Scoot").

* Once your dog does this movement with you, teach him to do it on his own.

* Use the dog's momentum to make the move while you stand still. Give the dog the "Scoot" command.

* Hold your feet still and twist your shoulder as far back as possible—your dog will naturally begin to position himself behind you.

* As soon as he takes that first step backward, tell him he's a genius and give him the treat!

* Remember, always give the treat in the position you want to reward—in this case, behind your ankles. (Who knew you'd end up so limber?)

* The moment he takes an extra step back on his own, praise, praise, praise, and reward him!

He'll soon figure out that you want him circling backward—a very flashy move. Circling behaviors like this come much more naturally to some breeds than others. Herding

Some dogs come up with their own moves!

breeds are notorious circlers, including Shelties and Corgis. Many Papillons also seem to have this trait.

Bow

Every dance routine needs a big finish, and doggie dancing is no exception. One of the best ways to end a routine is with a bow, of course.

Once you've finished your routine, take a bow.

❋ Have your dog standing.

❋ Hold a treat between his toes, so he has to pull his nose back a little to grab it.

❋ Praise him and give him the treat!

❋ Gradually shape the behavior by moving the treat toward his chest until he puts his front legs on the ground with his adorable rump in the air.

Be aware that "Bow" sounds a lot like "Down," and the motions are similar to the "Lie down" command. Many people select a different word for "Bow," such as "Curtsey."

Although you may never get to the more elaborate tricks, go ahead and try dancing with your dog—even if it's only to the radio. We humans express our emotions and our softer side when we dance. Your dog will be thrilled to share that part of you, as you dance across the floor together!

As Good As Disneyland?

If you have an active dog, and you've played the games in this chapter, I know you've got one happy dog on your hands. He may even think he's on vacation at Disneyland!

But life isn't all about action. Sometimes, it's a good idea to use our brains in a more mellow way. The next chapter is for the dog and human who need a little breather.

Sitting Pretty:

Chapter 4

Games You Can Play Without Leaving Your Living Room Chair

Some days we just can't make the living room into an agility course. Sometimes, our minds are too full to choreograph a musical number for our dog. Happily, our little dogs can still enjoy their time with us and be entertained. One of the best things about having a little dog is that we don't need to be jocks. (And even the athletes among us want a little down time some days.)

This chapter is full of things to do when you've already had too much to do. It's for the day when you need to sit back in your chair, but your little buddy still needs to have some fun.

Let's Play Fetch

The simplest and easiest way to entertain most dogs is to play fetch. All you have to do is throw a ball or toy. He'll run clear across the living room, grab it, and bring it back to you. He'll have a blast, and you don't even need to miss an episode of *Law & Order*.

Just 10 minutes a day of playing a rigorous game of living room fetch will make your little dog noticeably healthier. He'll get the aerobic exercise he needs to be healthy and live a long and good life. Just play until his little tongue is hanging from his mouth, and he's panting like any athlete.

The Give Command

"Fetch" is a game of give and take. While it's fine for your dog to just drop the toy at your feet, it's more fun for you both if he gently hands you the toy. If you ever want to use "Fetch" for something useful (such as giving you your keys), or if you want to compete in obedience, your dog needs a "Give" command.

If a Happy Fetcher Stops Fetching

If your dog normally loves to fetch, but he stops playing, take him to his veterinarian right away. Small dogs are notorious for having dental problems. If your dog has stopped fetching his beloved ball or has stopped chewing on his favorite chewy toy, that's a sign that his teeth probably hurt. Take him in and have him checked!

To Teach Give

* Your dog may teach himself. When he runs to you with his toy, turn your face away and hold out your hand. Most dogs will drop the toy in your outstretched hand. Tell your clever dog, "Good give!" and toss the toy as his reward!

* If he has no idea what you are asking, gently hold his head and take the toy from his mouth. Again, tell him "Good give!" and throw it again. As soon as your dog realizes that he gets to chase the toy after he hands it to you, he'll enjoy the game even more!

Teaching Fetch

Most dogs will naturally fetch objects, but not all dogs do. You can teach your dog to fetch, and he can play the game as happily as a natural fetcher. However, all dogs need to learn the Fetch command, even if they're natural fetchers.

If you're doing competitive obedience work or participating in a fetching sport like Flyball, your dog must understands that he always must fetch the object. Even if it's metal and tastes a little funny. Even if there's a toy on the floor he'd rather play with.

Here are two ways to teach your dog how to fetch an obedience dumbbell: the clicker method and a "shaping" method. Please notice that these are gentle, happy techniques. No dog should endure pain and suffering learning to fetch— and they don't need to!

Before You Teach Fetch

Lots of people report that their dogs hate to learn fetch. What the dog really doesn't like is all the contact with his face that's part and parcel of the exercise. Think about it: The dog is holding his dumbbell (or other object) and, all of a sudden, his owner's hands are swooping toward his face. To a dog, especially a small dog, that feels dangerous!

So, before you train the Fetch, be sure your dog is comfortable and enjoys having his face touched. (Read over the "Collapsing Tunnel" section of Chapter 3.)

The Clicker Fetch

This technique is all about fun, but before you start you'll need to have some understanding of clicker training. (See sidebar in Chapter 2: "What Is Clicker Training.")

Some dogs naturally love to fetch (even if the stick is bigger than they are!).

* Put the dumbbell down.
* When your dog sniffs it, click and treat.
* Continue to up the ante, as he touches it, mouths it, picks it up (Yes! Treat! Click!). Give the behavior the name "Fetch!"
* Once he understands the concept, throw the dumbbell a short distance and ask him to fetch.

Clicker training is all about rewarding small increments of behavior. I've seen this technique work very quickly and effectively with dogs. It's also a very good way for a shy or sensitive dog to learn to fetch.

The Shaping Fetch

Some dogs could spend eternity without ever deciding to spontaneously pick up the dumbbell. For them, the shaping method works best.

* *Gently* place the dumbbell in the dog's mouth. (You *have* followed the advice about getting the dog used to having his face touched, or this isn't fun or fair to the dog!)
* Then quickly say "Give" and give the dog a treat! He's great! He'll let go of the dumbbell to take the treat.

Don't turn fetch into a game of keep-away.

Is Your Dog Playing Keep-Away Instead of Retrieve?

For Fetch to be fun, it has to be a game for two. When the dog keeps the toy and expects you to chase him, this game quickly loses its fascination for many people.

If you have a keep-away artist, don't let him set the rules, or you're stuck. So, unless you think it's fun to chase a dog who will always be faster than you are, end the game until he brings the ball back. Turn your head as he stands there out of reach, mocking you. Hold out your hand for him to bring the toy to you. If you don't chase him, he'll figure out that if he wants to keep playing, he has to bring back the ball to you. He can learn to play nice!

On the other side of the equation, who in the world decided it was funny to pretend to throw a ball for a dog but really keep it? You don't like it when he plays keep-away, and he's equally frustrated when you pretend to throw a ball but keep it. You need to play nice, too!

* Over time, have the dog hold the dumbbell for longer and longer times. Begin to hold the dumbbell an inch (2 cm) away from his mouth, so he can reach for it.
* Once he reaches happily and eagerly for the dumbbell, put just one corner of the dumbbell on the ground, and have him fetch it.
* Put the entire dumbbell on the ground.
* Let go of the dumbbell, with your hand an inch (2 cm) away.
* Slowly and patiently build up the increments so that your dog learns to fetch the dumbbell reliably. Reward his successes each step of the way!

Whether you use the clicker method or the shaping method, this is usually a patient exercise for patient people. However, once your dog truly understands that retrieving is a command that's followed, and not just a spontaneous game that he sometimes plays, then you'll have a dog you can rely on. That's the dog who will pick up the pen you dropped, or go golfing with you.

Reluctant Fetchers

Some small breeds love to retrieve, including Toy and Miniature Poodles (who are descendants of retrieving dogs, after all), most of the terrier breeds, Dachshunds, Bichons Frise, and Papillons (who seem to love every sport on the planet). These dogs usually don't need any prompting: Throw something, and they will chase it.

But while some dogs like to chase and retrieve almost anything, others don't. For most of these dogs, it's about finding the right toy. Take your dog to the pet supply store and let him pick his own toys; you'll waste a lot less money buying toys he doesn't use. Let him sniff and check things out. He'll tell you which toy he wants!

At my house, the favorite toys are all stuffed animals with squeakers in them, which the dogs play with for hours at a time. When two dogs are squeaking their toys at once, it reminds me of the doggie version of "Dueling Banjos."

Demonstrating Fetch to a Disinterested Fetcher

Some dogs must be shown how to fetch. This can be especially true of rescue dogs who were adopted later in life. These poor little guys have long forgotten how to play. Happily, most dogs will pick up on the idea of fetch if they see another dog playing the game. If you don't have another dog, a human will do in a pinch. If you throw the toy, and the dog just sits there, *you* run and pick the toy up, toss it in the air, and generally act ecstatic. *Wow!* You got to play with the toy! Lucky, lucky you!

Some dogs become very attached to a certain toy.

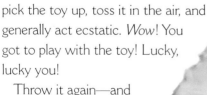

Throw it again—and retrieve it again. Most dogs will decide to join in the fun. You're reminding them of playing with their littermates. You've become an honorary dog.

However, a small number of

What To Do When Your Dog's One and Only Favorite Toy Is Nearing the End of Its Life

Some dogs are obsessed by just one toy. No matter what you do, nothing else interests them. This brings up a real issue: What do you do when the toy is completely, totally, and irreparably worn out?

Lizzie's experience with The Pig provides one answer. Lizzie was a wonderful, wise little Maltese-Poodle mix my sister-in-law adopted from a local shelter. Like many dogs adopted as adults, Lizzie really didn't like toys much. There was one exception: Lizzie absolutely loved her little rubber squeaky pig. She'd play fetch games with The Pig. She'd take The Pig on car trips with her. She loved him with a maternal gleam in her eye.

My sister-in-law tried for years to get Lizzie interested in other toys, but the dog would have none of it. Over time, The Pig became just a little limp bit of rubber of indistinguishable color. It was pretty nasty. My sister-in-law bought Lizzie identical rubber pigs to replace it, but Lizzie wasn't interested. She knew those imposters weren't The Pig.

My brother saw a show about lambs, and how farmers would bond surrogate moms who had lost their babies to orphaned lambs by wrapping the new lamb in the skin of the lamb that had died. The surrogate mom smelled her baby's scent, and allowed the orphan to nurse. Soon, the mom treated the orphan lamb as her own—a happy ending for lonely sheep.

So, my brother wrapped a brand new pig toy with the remaining remnants of The Pig. Lizzie sniffed—and it worked. After a few days, the old Pig remnants were removed, and what emerged was a new, cleaner, intact version of The Pig that lasted to the end of Lizzie's long and happy life.

If your dog is absolutely obsessed by just one toy, be sure to buy extra versions of the toy, and use the orphan lamb idea to make the transition if necessary.

dogs just don't like this fetching nonsense. These dignified little dogs, like Shih Tzu and Pekingese, will look at you like you are a lunatic. They seem to think, "You threw the toy away, you go pick it up." Other perfectly delightful things are described throughout this book that you can do with your dog if he doesn't like to fetch—some of them are included later in this chapter.

If your dog is not interested in fetching, don't force the issue.

Simple (and Not-So-Simple) Fetching Games

For dogs who love to fetch, here are some games to play.

Game #1: Help the Clumsy Owner

If you're like me, you drop stuff. A lot. If I drop food, I don't worry—my dogs will clean it up for me. But that's not this trick. This trick is about dropping stuff that's not edible. Things like pens, pieces of paper, envelopes I'm bringing in from the mail: all the detritus of my life. Your trained dog can pick these items up for you.

When I drop something, I ask Radar or Pogo to fetch it and bring it to me—as long as it isn't edible, they'll do it every time. That's because they know and understand the Fetch command, and have learned that "Fetch" means "pick up the object, bring it to me, and hold it until I say to give."

Continue to practice Fetch with your dog, and soon you'll be able to ask him to pick up items you've dropped.

Game #2: Putting Toys Away

This is a fun variation of fetch. Once your dog knows how to pick things up, show him where you want to put things away. In addition to Fetch, your dog has to know Drop It.

Teaching Drop It

* Have your dog fetch a toy.
* Hold a treat in one hand, gently take the toy from your dog's mouth, and say, "Drop it."
* Once your dog understands "Drop it," ask him to drop items specific places.
* Tell him to pick up the ducky, walk over to the toy basket with him, and tell him "Drop it." And then he gets a big treat!
* Try it with the panda bear. And the froggie. You get the idea—tidying up is fun. (I might have a tidier house if someone gave me a treat every time I picked up my stuff!).

Game #3: Playing Golf

My Papillon, Radar, knows how to "play golf"—his job is to make the putt. Like most guys, he loves the game! You can play indoors with a child's golf set, or you can bring your little guy out to the golf course if you happen to play.

* Play fetch with soft, foam practice golf balls.
* Create a target from a paper plate and place it on the floor.
* Once your dog has the golf ball in his mouth, walk over to the paper plate, point to it, and say, "Drop it."
* Practice until he understands the parts of the game, then you can give a command for the whole exercise: "Make par!"
* Roll the ball, say, "Make par," and he should deliver it to the paper plate.
* Cut the paper plate down to smaller and smaller sizes, until it's small enough to fit in a golf-ball hole.
* Point to the target in the hole before you ask your dog to "Make par" so that he knows what to do.

Game #4: Family Holiday Drawing

You don't have to be a highly trained retrieving dog to be valuable to the family. This game, invented by my brother for his Malti-Poo, Lizzie, allows your dog to choose names for a holiday gift exchange.

* Put the names of your family on slips of paper, and put them in a big paper grocery bag.
* Toss your dog's favorite toy into the bag (make sure he's been playing with it so it's nice and slimy).
* After your dog retrieves his favorite toy, have the members of your family call your dog.
* Whoever he approaches peels the name stuck to the toy, and that's who they buy a gift for.
* Keep throwing in the toy and having him pull it out until all the names are gone.

Okay, maybe it's a little gross, but it's fair—your dog is above reproach; he won't play favorites among the relatives!

Game #5: Inventing Their Own Fetching Games

Some dogs invent their own fetch games. When Pogo can't engage my other dogs or the cat in a fun game, he'll grab a small toy in his mouth, throw it, and chase it. Sometimes he even throws it and catches it mid-air. If you provide fun toys for your dog, there will be times he can amuse himself.

Some dogs invent their own fetching games.

Puzzle Toys

While I'm writing this chapter, my dogs are playing with puzzle toys. I can't take time out right now to play a game of fetch, but they still need a little fun. Puzzle toys provide interaction with dogs. They're great for those times when you're out of the house, or for those times when you just can't amuse your dog at the moment. Many kinds of puzzle toys are available online or in pet stores. As with any toy, you should make sure they are the appropriate size for your dog, and make sure there are no parts that might potentially choke your pup.

Stuffable Rubber Toys

Cylindrical-shaped rubber-like toys with a hollow center can be filled with a smear of peanut butter, a little kibble, and corked at the top with some string cheese. This is astoundingly interesting to a dog! The toy eventually takes on the smell of the food, so long after their little tongues have dislodged the food, they're still interested.

Treat-Dispensing Toys

Plastic toys are available that dispense treats as your dog nudges them. There's even a complicated toy that also allows you to record your voice. So, you can be cooing to your dog while he noses the toy around the floor, nudging the treats out. If your dog doesn't like the plastic toys, you can also find the same type of treat-dispensing toy in a plush version.

Plush Puzzles

Your dog might enjoy plush toys that contain little toys inside for the dog to remove. These are fun for the dog who loves stuffed toys and loves getting things out of small spaces.

Puzzle toys can keep your dog occupied and chase away boredom.

How Did He Do That?!

Chapter 5

Tricks to Impress Your Friends and Amuse Your Dog

If you played any of the games in the previous chapters, you've already taught your dog tricks. When you played nose games like "Which Hand" and the "Shell Game," you were doing tricks. The moves for Canine Freestyle are really just tricks set to music. When you ask your dog to pick up a pen you dropped, what is that but a trick?

Anatomy of a Trick

In this chapter, you'll learn some new tricks. More important, you'll learn the anatomy of teaching a trick. That will allow you to teach your dog an endless number of practical or fun behaviors, and then string them together to make them even more entertaining.

Here's what you need to know about teaching tricks: capturing a behavior and shaping a behavior.

Practice

Practice makes perfect—but not too much. Try to practice each new trick every day, but keep your training sessions short—about 10 minutes at a time. Always end a training session with success, rewarding the dog for what he's learned that day. Remember to practice tricks he knows well to keep his confidence high!

Capturing a Behavior: Leap in the Air

The simplest trick is to "capture" and name a behavior that your dog does naturally. Clickers are ideal for capturing that moment you want to mark in your dog's mind.

A great example is teaching a dog to leap into the air on command. My friend Leah does this move with her Australian Shepherd, Flare, as part of their dancing with dogs routine.

If you have a dog who loves to bounce in the air, recognize it!

* Use your clicker and click at the instant your dog leaps into the air. That click is a marker, telling your dog that you want that behavior. (It can also work to say "Good" instead of giving a treat, but when a dog is doing something as absorbing as leaping into the air, he'll likely notice the distinctive sound of a clicker long before he'd ever notice your word.)
* Give your dog a treat.
* Repeat every time you see him perform that behavior: Leap, *click*, treat. Leap, *click*, treat.
* Soon your dog will figure out that when he leaps, you click.
* Then add the command word—when he leaps, say, "Leap!" (or "Fly" or "Anti-gravity," whatever word you choose) and then *click*.
* Once he associates the word "Leap" with the

You can reward your dog for jumping in order to capture that behavior.

behavior, you can say "Leap" and he will!

You can use this method for other behaviors your dog offers naturally: Catch them with a *click*, reward, and (eventually) name the trick.

Shaping: Ride a Skateboard

When Riley, a Cardigan Welsh Corgi, hears the words, "Let's go skating!" he takes a running jump at his own personal skateboard. He lands on the board with all four paws, the momentum of his effort carrying the happy dog forward several yards. When the skateboard slows down, he reaches down with his short little back leg, and pushes so the speed builds up again.

Riley's owner taught him to do this with a combination of capturing the behavior with clicker training, and gentle shaping. *Shaping* is showing the dog (in doggie terms) what you want him to do. It might be *gently* placing him into a position, or luring him into a position with a treat. This contrasts with clicker training, in which you reward a dog for a behavior that he offers by himself.

Start by capturing the behavior:

* Put the skateboard on the ground.
* Begin clicking and rewarding any interaction your dog has with the skateboard.
* If your dog sniffs near the board, *click* and treat.
* If he touches it with his nose, *click* and treat.
* If he puts his foot on the skateboard, *click* and treat.

More than likely, you'd have to wait a long time before your dog thinks of putting all four feet on the skateboard. That's where some gentle shaping helps:

* Show your dog very gently where you want his feet.
* Get him comfortable putting one paw on the board.
* Slowly work up to two paws, and then three, and finally four. Each step along

the way, *click* and treat his progress!

❋ Each behavior (paw) is built up separately and rewarded.

❋ Be sure he feels safe and secure on the stationary skateboard before you move it.

❋ Once he's secure, move the board just a fraction of an inch, and then reward the dog. Many dogs love the motion, and quickly start pushing themselves along!

Chains of behavior, like riding the skateboard, take longer to train than a single move, like the jump. They take a combination of gentle, positive teaching techniques, such as clicking when the dog offers a behavior as well as gently putting one foot on the skateboard and praising and treating the dog when he's in the correct position.

Breaking Down a Trick: Pick a Card

Teach you little dog to do a card trick. Have an "assistant" (maybe a child or friend) pull out a card from the deck and hand it to you. Say a magic word, and lay the card face down among several other cards from the deck. Then ask your dog to find it.

Magic? No—scent discrimination. But this trick involves a complicated set of behaviors. Here are the steps your dog must learn to do this magic trick:

❋ Make sure your dog has a reliable fetch (see Chapter 4).

❋ Once he knows Fetch, you can teach your dog to pick out the scent of an article you've touched and ignore others.

❋ Tying a playing card down to a board.

❋ Then, place a card you've touched next to it.

❋ Tell your dog to Fetch—only one card can possibly come back with him.

❋ Your dog will try to figure out what it is that makes one card move, while the other remains on the board.

❋ Eventually you'll see the light bulb go off: The card that smells like you is the one to bring back!

❋ Over time, add more cards you haven't touched, but once your dog understands the concept, it won't matter much how many objects are out there.

This is the same way a dog learns to retrieve a dumbbell for obedience exercises. Interestingly, even if your dog can retrieve a dumbbell, he would still have to essentially learn the entire exercise over to substitute for cards. *Dogs don't generalize training concepts.* You'll have to train the card trick from the beginning, just as you did for the dumbbell exercise. Your dog will figure it out, but he'll still need time and patience while he's learning it.

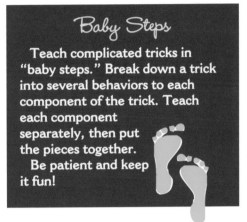

Baby Steps

Teach complicated tricks in "baby steps." Break down a trick into several behaviors to each component of the trick. Teach each component separately, then put the pieces together.

Be patient and keep it fun!

Tricks for Your Little Genius

Now that you know the basic components of capturing a behavior, shaping, and breaking down a trick, the sky's the limit for what you can teach your little guy!

Trick #1: Flashcard

This trick will leave your audience thinking that your dog can read, but he's really just following his nose to a hidden treat.

* Teach him a special word that means "treat" to him. Let's assume that word is "please."
* Place a treat on a blank flashcard.
* Say "Please" and let your dog get the treat off the blank flashcard. (It won't take long for him to love this command!)
* Once he's getting the treat from the top of the card, put the treat under the card and say "Please."
* After he's figured out he's using his nose to find the treat, you're in!
* Write "Lassie" on a flashcard, and place a treat under it.
* Ask him to "find Lassie, please"—all he will hear is his command "Please."
* He'll be off to find his treat—which happens be under the card with "Lassie" on it.

You can also try this with math flashcards, and impress your friends with your little dog's ability to add and subtract!

The Joys of Hand Signals

We talked about using hand signals in the "Dancing with Dogs" section of Chapter 3. It's easy to teach hand signals for commands like Sit and Down. They certainly impress people when you're doing even simple commands.

Hand signals can also add to the joy of having a dog. When my Papillon, Pogo, visits the hospital as a therapy dog, sometimes kids try to give him commands. I unobtrusively give Pogo a hand signal, and he seemingly does just what the child asked for. It's so wonderful to see the look of joy on a small child's face when he says "Sit" or "Lie down," and the dog does exactly what he asks. And Pogo doesn't tell that he's really following my cues.

Trick #2: Jump Through a Hoop

Once your dog has learned how to jump over something on command, he can learn to jump through a hoop. The hoop can be any size that the dog can jump through comfortably—most big-box toy stores have hula hoops that work well.

Remember, though, dogs don't generalize, so you must go through the following steps:

If your dog does not know how to jump a hurdle, instructions can be found in Chapter 3.

* Hold the hoop upright, with the bottom of the hoop on the ground.
* Hold a treat on the other side, and give your dog his "Jump" command.
* As he goes through the hoop, praise him.
* Give him the treat when he finishes.
* Over time, raise the height of the hoop.
* You can also start using smaller and smaller hoops, so your dog is eventually jumping through a little tiny hoop high in the air.

The kids can help teach your dog to jump through a hoop.

Trick #3: Play the Piano

My friend Gail's Papillons, Mia and Diva, love to put on a show by playing a duet on a toy piano. This is a great clicker-trained trick. You can find inexpensive toy pianos at any of the big toy stores.

* Make a big production of showing the new piano to your dog, and have your clicker in hand.

* As soon as your dog shows interest in the piano, click, and treat.

* If you've done any other clicker training with your dog, he'll quickly know the drill: Once he figures out what he has to do with the piano, he'll keep getting those clicks and treats!

* Each time your dog touches the piano, click and treat.

* Gradually up the ante: Only click when your dog paws at the piano.

* After the dog consistently paws at the piano, only click when the dog paws at the keys and makes noise.

* Once he's doing the desired behavior, label the behavior. ("Good symphony!")

It won't take long at all before your little Chihuahua Chopin or Maltese Mozart is playing away.

Putting on a Show

Think about taking all the clever things your dog does, adding some flair, and entertaining some people (as well as yourself). Make it a production! Have fun! This may be a great way to start working in schools or hospitals.

Trick #4: Stick Out Your Tongue

This trick is easy to teach!

* Hold a treat just a little bit in front of your dog's nose.
* When he reaches out his tongue to get it, say, "Good tongue" and reward.
* Gradually hold the treat farther and farther out, so your dog gets used to reaching for the treat with his tongue.
* Then, see if your dog has learned to associate the word "tongue" with the action of sticking out his tongue.
* Hold the treat, say "Tongue," then reward and give him the treat when he complies!
* Gradually wait longer and longer to reward, and soon you'll have a dog that sticks out his tongue when you say "Tongue."

Some little dogs have surprisingly big tongues. It's very entertaining to see the big tongue unfold when the owner says, "Stick out your tongue!" Kids love it (adults secretly do, too).

Stick out your tongue is an easy trick to teach.

Trick #5: Bring Me a Tissue

Achoo! You just sneezed, and you need a tissue *now!* Not to worry—as long as you train your dog to do this trick. This trick is taught in two parts: fetch the tissue, and fetch the tissue that's sitting in a box.

❉ Review the section on teaching "Fetch" in Chapter 4.

❉ Ball up a tissue so it's easy for your dog to grab, throw it, and say, "Fetch."

❉ Keep playing Fetch until your dog is doing it reliably even with an edible tissue!

❉ Once he's fetching the balled-up tissue, put one flat on the ground and ask him to fetch.

❉ With the tissue on the floor, say "Fetch" and, when he picks it up, say "Achoo! Good Achoo!" as he brings the tissue back to you.

❉ Gradually move the tissue farther away; then, put the tissue in the box.

Dogs love this trick and will quickly be grabbing the tissue from the box. Just remember to teach this trick one step at a time, in baby steps, so you don't confuse your dog. After all, becoming a trained medical professional (well, a tissue retriever) takes a little time.

Trick #6: Crawl on Your Stomach

It's fun to teach little dogs to crawl.

❉ Sit on the ground with your feet flat on the floor and your knees bent, creating a little tunnel for your dog.

❉ Lure your dog under your knees with a treat. Be sure your knees are up high enough to let your dog through, but low enough to require your dog to crawl.

❉ Tell him "Good crawl!" as he crawls through your legs.

❉ Once he's crawling confidently under your knees, gradually put your knees higher and higher, rewarding him for staying in the crawl position.

Eventually you can use the "crawl" command without using your legs.

Crawling on his stomach might be a fun trick to learn.

Trick #7: Say Your Prayers

Like many tricks, "Say Your Prayers" is the combination of two behaviors. Each behavior by itself is simple: Put together, they look complicated. "Say Your Prayers" combines "Paws Up" and "Sad Dog." The goal is to have a dog who puts his cute little face on his paws—which looks sad, even though he's happily, greedily waiting for his reward!

* Put out a footstool or other object that is comfortable for your small dog to put his front feet up on. (People with large dogs usually use a chair, but that doesn't work for a pint-sized pooch.)
* Coax him to put his paws up on the footstool.
* Tell him "Good Paws Up!" when he does.
* Work on that half of the trick until the dog understands it completely.
* Then work on the other half of the trick: Sad dog.
* When your dog is lying down, hold a treat to the floor.
* When his chin rests on the floor to get the treat from your hand, tell him "Good Sad Dog!" (or click the behavior).
* Combine the two behaviors when he understands both separately: "Paws Up!" quickly followed by "Sad Dog!"
* When the dog is in the "Prayer" position, say "Good Prayers!"
* Reward the prayer position, and soon your dog will be offering his prayers on a regular basis.

When he's wagging his tail, we'll never know if he's thinking about the treat that's coming his way—or if he's just feeling the power of prayer.

You'll get ideas for tricks just by watching your dog.

Trick #8: Play Basketball

So, your dog might not be tall enough to get drafted for the NBA, but the two of you can play for the love of the game.

This game works best with a dog who loves to play fetch, and knows how to Drop It (See page 79).

* Play with a small, soft ball that your dog can easily hold in his mouth.
* Rig up a basketball hoop. (Okay—a Pomeranian doesn't actually need a regulation-sized NBA hoop. A child's toy, or any basket-shaped "hoop" will do.)
* Start with the hoop at floor level.
* Show your dog that you want him to drop the ball in the hoop by demonstrating it yourself.
* Have him approach the basket and ask him to "Drop it."

Gradually, make the hoop taller, until he has to reach up to make the basket.

Once he understands the game, this is a blast! Throw the dog the "basketball" and tell him to make the hoop—the Championship season has been saved!

Once you start teaching your dog tricks, you won't want to stop. You'll get ideas from all kinds of places, from television shows to just watching your dog. It's a bonding experience that will last a lifetime.

Have fun!

Party Hearty!

Chapter 6

Celebrations and Parties With Your Little Dog

Nothing is more joyful than watching small dogs play together. They bow down on their front legs, tails wagging in the air, then explode in a gleeful chase. They wrestle, they run, they bark.

Little dogs get too few opportunities for fun. After all, it's not a good idea for little dogs to play with big ones. Just an errant paw from a big, sweet dog can permanently injure your little guy. And we won't even think what happens if a larger dog has evil intent.

So, unless your town has a small-dog park, your little dog doesn't get to hang out because it's just too dangerous.

What's a pet-lover to do?

Why, invite friends over, of course! It's time to have a play day!

Special Events

Here are some special events that practically scream for a party:

New puppy: Have a shower for your friend's new family member. Guests can bring gifts for the youngster.

Birthday: Celebrate either your dog's "belly button" birthday or the anniversary of his adoption, if you don't know the date he was born.

Christmas/Hanukkah: This sure beats the office party! How about everyone bringing cookies, and doing a cookie exchange? (Dog cookies, of course!)

Halloween: Have a costume contest.

Of course, you and your dog are so much fun, you don't really *need* a reason to throw a party.

Whom to Invite

Invite the nice neighbor dogs, or the small dogs from puppy kindergarten. You could even post an invitation at a local doggie day care or obedience training facility.

I go to a wonderful Papillon Play Day that Gail "the Papillon Goddess" has at her home every month. She just posted a play day on a nation-wide Internet e-mail list for Papillon lovers. She's been holding the monthly events for 6 years. We've welcomed new people and new puppies, mourned some losses, and all become friends.

So, don't be shy! Your dog needs buddies, and it's your job to find them.

Give friends a call, drop them an e-mail, or send a fancy invitation. I promise that people will be delighted.

The Big Event

Make the event as snazzy or relaxed as suits you. Parties with themes can be great fun. How about holding a "Black tie and tails" party where everyone comes in formal wear? Or a "dog dreams" party with decorations of bones, cats to chase, and squirrels? A costume party can be a blast, with humans and dogs both dressed. (Imagine the woman and her Pug arriving as Miss Piggy and

You can have a contest for the best costume.

Kermit, or two Chihuahuas as Chip & Dale.)

If you're not so much a do-it-yourself type, but still like the idea of decorations or dogs in birthday hats, check out Dog Birthdays and Parties at www.dogbirthdaysandparties.com or Tail Waggin' Celebrations at www.tailwagging.com. Both sites have products to buy, party planning tips, festive recipes and, yes, dog party hats.

Inside Versus Outside

Let's be brutally honest for a moment: Small dogs are notorious leg-lifters. Even dogs who are well-behaved at home are likely to go on a peeing spree when they find themselves in a strange place with new dogs. You'll need to plan for this problem.

The easiest solution is to hold the party outside, and let the dogs pee to their heart's content. If you're holding the party inside, keep the dogs in a room where you don't have heirlooms that can't stand up to a little pee. Show your guests where you've got the clean-up supplies and ask them to watch their dogs.

And then remember—life's too short to stress over the small stuff!

Don't Have the Space for a Party?

Check with a local doggie day care. They're usually empty on weekends and may be delighted to rent out their facility to you.

A local park can also be a good location. However, be sure some system of secure fencing is in place! One solution is to have everyone bring exercise pens, and just clip them all together.

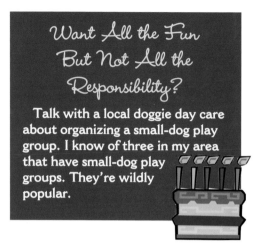

Want All the Fun But Not All the Responsibility?

Talk with a local doggie day care about organizing a small-dog play group. I know of three in my area that have small-dog play groups. They're wildly popular.

Snacks can be as simple as Cheerios in a bowl, your dog's favorite liver treats, or even crunchy snacks like carrots. Distribute water bowls around the area. Have clean-up supplies ready to go for the obvious reasons.

Remember, each dog will arrive with two or three people. They might appreciate some food, too.

Cookies

You can also choose to get more elaborate and bake cookies. My friend Leah is the Pied Piper of the dog set. The animals see their favorite "cookie lady," and they follow her anywhere.

These fish cookies are a big favorite. The dogs love their taste. They're also softer than most dog cookies, which makes them ideal for training and for little dogs in general.

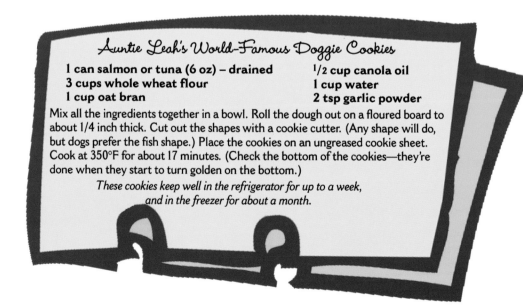

Auntie Leah's World-Famous Doggie Cookies

1 can salmon or tuna (6 oz) – drained
3 cups whole wheat flour
1 cup oat bran

1/2 cup canola oil
1 cup water
2 tsp garlic powder

Mix all the ingredients together in a bowl. Roll the dough out on a floured board to about 1/4 inch thick. Cut out the shapes with a cookie cutter. (Any shape will do, but dogs prefer the fish shape.) Place the cookies on an ungreased cookie sheet. Cook at 350°F for about 17 minutes. (Check the bottom of the cookies—they're done when they start to turn golden on the bottom.)

These cookies keep well in the refrigerator for up to a week,
and in the freezer for about a month.

Cake

Is it your dog's birthday? Certainly you should bake him a cake.

The traditional birthday cake isn't chocolate—it's a hamburger cake. This recipe has many versions; this one evolved in my friend Leah's kitchen over the years.

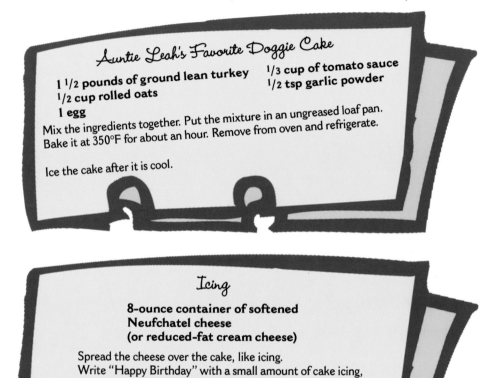

Auntie Leah's Favorite Doggie Cake

1 1/2 pounds of ground lean turkey
1/2 cup rolled oats
1 egg
1/3 cup of tomato sauce
1/2 tsp garlic powder

Mix the ingredients together. Put the mixture in an ungreased loaf pan. Bake it at 350°F for about an hour. Remove from oven and refrigerate.

Ice the cake after it is cool.

Icing

8-ounce container of softened Neufchatel cheese (or reduced-fat cream cheese)

Spread the cheese over the cake, like icing.
Write "Happy Birthday" with a small amount of cake icing, or put up small baby carrots (which look like candles), the tips dipped in the icing so they look like melting wax candles.

Gift Bags

Take-home gift bags can be almost as much fun as the party. It's easy to find cute, doggie-themed bags, or you can stencil a bag with bone designs. Pack the bag with doggie cookies and some squeaky toys. (Look for very inexpensive toys at dollar stores. I've also found great small-dog sized toys in the bargain areas of discount stores.)

Games

Compatible dogs are happy to just play. They only hate the part where they have to wait around while someone reads the rules. Still, especially at puppy showers and holiday parties, it can be fun to have a little bit of competition. (Give the winners a dog toy.) One of the best parts about having dogs is that it gives adult humans a chance to be silly.

Game #1: Popcorn Toss

Owners stand 6 feet (1.8 m) away from their dogs, and then throw popcorn

for the dog to catch, mid-air. The dog who catches the most popcorn in 3 minutes wins. (Remember, air-popped, no butter on the popcorn.)

Game #2: Bobbing for Hotdogs

Put baby hotdogs (from the baby-food section of the supermarket) in a tub of water. The dog who eats the most hot dogs wins.

Game #3: Best Trick Contest

You be the judge! Ask your friends to show off their dogs' abilities with tricks, and you give the winner a prize. (Of course, anyone who's read this book should clean up in a contest like that one!).

Bullies

It's bound to happen sooner or later. You will have a dog-guest at your party who's a bully. He (or she!) will snark and nip and make all the other dogs afraid to play. The bully's owner thinks that her dog is just adorable—Little Hannibal just has his own style of play, and she's sure that the other dogs (who are cowering in the corner) love him, deep in their hearts.

Sorry! As hostess, you need to tactfully intervene. If you don't, the other dogs and humans will miss out on a lot of fun.

Don't let any of the dogs become bullies—parties should be fun!

Game #4 Pin the Tail on the Pug (For Your Human Guests!)

This is the same game as "Pin the Tail on the Donkey," but with a twist—well, a twisted tail. Put up a big picture of a Pug with one detail missing: his tail! Blindfold the player, turn her in a circle three times, and hand her a paper Pug tail with a piece of tape attached. The dizzy, blind-folded person who can come closest to taping the Pug tail in the correct spot wins a prize.

Some things only dogs can do for other dogs. By creating play opportunities for your little guy with dogs his size, you are giving him a precious gift. As you see these little dogs become friends—and you become friends with their humans—you'll be so glad you made the effort!

Partygoers can show off their best trick.

Part 2

Stepping Out

Chapter 7

Six Feet, Two Hearts: Walking, Hiking, Jogging, or Biking With Your Small Dog

You may be a fitness fanatic, or you may be considering adding activities like hiking, biking, and jogging to your life. Those of us who have little dogs can find a way to get active with our dogs. This chapter will give you some new ideas about the oldest activity with dogs: going for a walk. Plus, if jogging, hiking, or biking are more your speed, there are plenty of tips for you, too!

Walking

Going for a walk with your dog offers you a glimpse of the magic of a wolf pack.

It doesn't matter that our dogs are small and unbearably cute. The relationship that we feel is the same as that in a pack. We're on the move together, sniffing out the creatures who've crossed our path, scanning the horizon for friend and foe, and absolutely committed to taking care of each other. Nothing is more bonding for a dog than a walk.

It's an activity that too few little dogs get to experience.

However, if you have a "yap dog" who snarks at every big dog who comes along, it's no fun to go for a walk. Also, other little dogs can't go far enough or fast enough to keep up with their more athletic owners. Some owners worry that their dog isn't safe on a walk. All these problems can be overcome.

For Starters, Good Leash Manners

If people on the street laugh and ask, "Are you walking your dog or is that dog walking you?" you probably already know you have a problem. You aren't communicating with your dog. He is on his own mission, and you (as the old dog-training expression goes) are just the "Dope on a Rope." Happily, some easy training—and one fabulous new gadget—can solve your walking problems. Follow these simple directions, and your dog will stop pulling on the leash. Honest.

Walking on a Loose Leash

* Your dog should be wearing a comfortable buckle or snap collar (not a choke collar) or a harness.
* Use a lightweight 4- or 6-foot (1.2- or 1.8-m) leash (not a flexi leash).
* Say, "Let's go" (or "Walkies" or whatever word suits you) and start walking.

Going for a walk can be the best exercise.

* If he pulls on the leash, turn in the other direction and say "Let's go!" the instant his leash tightens.
* If he runs out and pulls in the new direction, turn and go a different way, saying, "Let's go!"
* The moment he's walking on a loose leash (not pulling), give him (an easily chewed) treat, and tell him he's a very, very good dog.

Very quickly, your dog will figure out that he will never, ever get where he wants to go if he pulls. On the other hand, keeping an eye on you is incredibly fun. Soon, he will be merrily walking on a loose leash!

Front-Attaching Harness

While you're in the process of leash training, you might consider buying a front-attaching harness. Rather than attaching the leash to the back of the harness (a design which actually encourages pulling), these harnesses attach at the front. As a result, when the dog pulls, the harness actually steers the dog toward you, rather than away. These harnesses are designed so that they don't pull on your dog's neck, so they're safer and gentler on a dog with a tendency to pull than a collar is. Another plus about having a harness that turns your dog toward you is that he can't focus on other dogs, which means he'll stop barking at every passing pooch. (You can also teach him to focus on you on command by training the Watch Me command, found in the Appendix.)

A few of these products are on the market, including the Easy Walk harness, the SENSE-ible harness, and the Front Lead harness. These harnesses can be found on the web and at many pet supply stores.

And remember, practice makes perfect. The more you walk

If your dog pulls on his harness, there are ways to solve the problem.

When Doing Right Feels Good

We live in hectic, overscheduled times, and sometimes we don't always give our canine companions the exercise they need. Sometimes the guilt can be overwhelming, like when I'm putting in 20-hour days to meet a deadline. That means that my dogs—who are usually busy enough to practically require Blackberries to keep track of their schedules—are bored, bored, bored. During these times, I'm convinced Pogo is plotting a revolution, and (after doing unspeakable things to my poor cat) will turn on me.

When the guilt gets too much, I break down and take a little time from writing to go for a walk with them. Just a short distance allows them to bounce at birds, wag their tails at neighbors, and sniff at mole hills.

When we return, they are immeasurably calmer. They aren't barking each time someone walks by. They aren't pouncing on Mews the cat. They aren't staring at me, wondering what I'm going to do for them.

The little walk relaxes me too, and helps clear my tired brain and focus. Sometimes, when we listen to the little voice that makes us feel guilty, we not only do the right thing, we actually do the thing that makes us feel good.

together, the better your dog will behave. Then you'll even have more fun on your walks. And who knows, walking your dog could just be the key to a healthier lifestyle for you. It was for me!

"Lift Up"

Some owners worry about taking their small dogs on walks, and rightly so. Larger, untrained dogs can be a danger to our petite pooches. Nine years ago, a large Lab-mix broke away from his owner and chased down Radar while we were on a walk. Luckily, I've trained all my dogs to jump into my arms using a Lift Up command.

Having a Lift up command for Radar undoubtedly saved his life. There's no way he could have escaped that big, fast dog on foot. It's a great thing to teach your little dog. Here's how:

* Every time you pick up your dog, simply say, "Lift up!" in a happy voice.
* Be sure to support your dog's body, so he feels comfortable when you pick him up.

❄ You dog will soon offer his body to be lifted when you say "Lift up." Some dogs stand rigidly. Others put their paws up on your leg. Others, like my Pogo, take matters in their own paws and leap up in your arms.

You might also choose a vest-style harness for your dog, so that you can grab the harness and hoist him to safety. My favorite brand is the Ruffwear Web Master harness (available at www.ruffwear.com). The large version of this harness was designed for service dogs who sometimes must be lifted over obstructions and into transport vehicles. This well-made harness has been proven durable and sturdy, yet lightweight and comfortable.

Jogging

For some activities, like jogging, an exceptionally athletic little dog will enjoy sharing the experience. For example, Border Terriers and Jack Russell Terriers both keep up with horses on fox hunts. Their long legs and athletic bodies make most of these dogs great jogging buddies. Some Whippets, Shelties, and some larger Papillons are other examples of small dogs who might have the ability and desire to jog with a human.

If you have a small-dog canine athlete, he still needs conditioning before taking on a full jogging route, just as you did. Start out with short distances and a slow pace. Build up gradually. If he's lagging behind, you're asking too

As long as your dog is built for it, jogging can keep you both in shape.

Backpacking Bowser

Your Pekingese might be more of an urban dog. The thought of getting his paws in mud—much less walking in it—isn't his idea of a good time. Not to worry—he has the perfect beast of burden: You! Dog backpacks allow you to comfortably carry a small dog on a hiking trip or a jog. Just be sure that, if you decide to do this, you purchase one that doesn't have your dog sitting upright, like a baby. That's very hard on a dog's back, especially for long-backed breeds who tend to have back problems.

much of him. Don't jog with a dog until he's about a year old, because too much repetitive motion can damage the growth plates in his legs. (Your young dog will be trying so hard to please you that he might not show you that he's uncomfortable until the damage is done.)

After you've waited until your dog is old enough, and conditioned him, you'll both enjoy the exercise together. No better running buddy exists than your active, athletic dog. And he won't let you turn into a couch potato—he'll bring you your Nikes and tell you it's time to run!

(Not) Born to Run

Most little dogs, even athletic, fit ones, aren't built for jogging. Years ago, there was a woman who used to run by my condo with her Miniature Pinscher. I know she thought she was doing good things for her dog. The dog did manage to keep up with her, but he was so bulked up he almost looked like he was stealing steroids from a major league ballplayer. If your little dog is overmuscled, he's being asked to do too much.

You can still take your little dog with you if you jog. Just as some strollers for new parents come in jogging models, you can find a jogging model for your pet stroller. He'll enjoy being with you, and you'll stay fit.

Hiking

Going for a walk with a dog is great, and hiking can be a slice of heaven. Your dog will show you things you'd never have noticed without that clever nose of his!

Lucky Eddie and the Bike Trailer

Eddie is a happy Corgi mix adopted by my friend Markie. He's definitely not built for speed, plus he's had some orthopedic problems, so running long or fast just isn't a possibility.

Markie really missed having Eddie with her when she'd go for bike rides, until one day she realized Eddie would be a perfect candidate for a bike trailer. Markie keeps Eddie's trailer attached to her bike, and the two of them love their rides together. "Eddie barks at me when I ride. I couldn't figure out at first why he'd bark sometimes and not others," says Markie. Then she figured it out: "Eddie always barks when we're going up hill. He's telling me he wants to go faster!" says Markie with a laugh. So she does her best to speed up. "He loves to feel the wind in his face."

Work on your "going for a walk" manners before going for a hike. You want him to walk along nicely, not pull you all over the trail.

Your little guy belongs on a leash when you're in the woods. Last summer, my dogs (along with some friends and their dogs) were hiking in the Oregon woods. My dogs are very well trained—but they smelled deer and probably bears. They were ready to hunt! I didn't trust them (who all have obedience titles) off their leashes. When we wandered by a tiny, shallow stream, suddenly Radar became excited. He jumped in the little stream and started digging in the silt. He reached down—and pulled a dead frog from the muck. He was so proud that he'd found dinner! I was glad for two things: that he was having so much fun, and that I'd taught him a reliable Drop It command so I didn't have to touch the thing!

If you're planning long hikes, be sure to get your dog in condition for the miles and the terrain. Consider getting him booties if he'll be walking on rough surfaces. Of course, don't forget that he'll need plenty of water along the way.

Do check to be sure that dogs are allowed where you're going. A surprising number of outdoor places prohibit dogs. Your Chihuahua isn't an imminent danger to wild birds or to elk herds, but the same "No Dogs Allowed" rules apply to your 6-pound (2.7 kg) dog as do to an Irish Wolfhound.

Bicycling

If you love riding your bike for miles at a time, you can share this activity with your little dog by getting a bicycle basket designed for pets. This clever product attaches to your bicycle handlebars and allows your dog to ride in safety and comfort. It includes a harness to keep your dog safely attached to the carrier. It even has a metal frame so, in case you have a spill on your bike, your dog still has some protection.

Find a safe carrier for your dog.

If you have a dog who's too big to fit in the basket, but isn't built for speed, consider getting a bicycle trailer designed for small children. They are widely available at department stores. They'll comfortably fit your small-to medium-sized dog, and are also a great alternative for bringing two or three toy-sized dogs with you on a ride.

Most dogs must be persuaded that riding in a basket or a trailer is a good idea. Introduce them to the new environment gradually. Place your dog in the rig, and give him a treat. Make sure he's comfortable before you start wheeling him around. Once he's accustomed to the space, add slow movement. Walk the bike and talk with him. Give him treats. When he's comfortable with that, start bicycling.

Remember, on the trip, he needs the same things you need. If you're riding in warm weather, bring water for him. If it's sunny, be sure he's shaded.

Take care of him, and you'll both have a blast!

Dieting With Your Dog: Exercising Together to Fitness

In the last year, I've lost just over 100 pounds (45 kg). I owe all my weight-loss success to my Papillon, Pogo. Like about half of American people and their pets, my dog and I were both overweight. Pogo needed to lose about a half-pound (.2 kg), the equivalent of 10 pounds (4.5 kg) worth of love handles on his small-dog frame. I obviously needed to lose a lot more.

Of course, I've always been better at giving advice to others than to implementing it myself. I'd put Pogo on a sensible diet, never considering one for myself. That changed when, after scarfing up his dinner, Pogo gave me a sad look that clearly asked, "Isn't there more?"

"You're just fine. You've had plenty," I lectured to him. Then I looked down at my heaping plate of spaghetti and had an epiphany. "Deborah, you are such a hypocrite," I said out loud. The next day, I was at my first Weight Watchers meeting.

Pogo and I are a great support system for each other. When it comes to weight loss, dog lovers have a leg up—make that four legs up—over people who don't have pets. In a year-long study at Northwestern University in Chicago, overweight people and their portly pooches received nutritional and exercise counseling. The core component of the program was daily walks for the people and their pets. A control group without dogs got the same program. Not only did the pet owners lose more weight, they were happier.

For those of us who were never jocks, other forms of exercise can be intimidating. I can't imagine going to a gym full of hard-bodies. For people like me, walking with our dogs is a Lycra-free zone of acceptance. Because we focus on our dogs rather than on ourselves, we give ourselves permission to take the risk of exercising our less than perfect bodies.

It's even okay if we seem a little silly to other people. When I wanted to step up my exercise, it was obvious that Pogo and I would go for long, vigorous walks. But I had a problem: My two older dogs weren't up for the demands of

If your dog is overweight, discuss an exercise routine with your vet.

Here's what to look for:

• Your dog's figure should have a definite waist. Even a breed like a Pug, with a naturally boxy build, should have an indent when you look down at the dog from above.

• The dog should also have a tuck-up—from the side, the tummy should lift up behind the rib cage.

• You should be able to feel your dog's ribs and spine. If you're feeling them through a layer of fat, it doesn't count!

Ask your veterinarian to honestly tell you if your buddy needs to be on a doggie diet. Some vets don't offer up the suggestion without being asked (probably because so many owners are so touchy about this subject), but all veterinarians will be able to tell you if your little buddy needs to cut down on calories and build up on exercise.

long power walks. My solution was to buy a pet stroller. I got a flashy red model with three wheels that looks just like a jogging stroller for kids. I let Goldie and Radar each walk as far as they feel comfortable, then put them in the stroller when they tire. Then Pogo and I pick up the pace. The older dogs love their rides in the sunshine while Pogo and I pant together on foot. I don't care when people giggle a little when they see us. My old dogs, my young dog, and I are all having a great time.

People who exercise with their dogs have fun, no matter what their level of fitness may be. "You don't grow to love the StairMaster. No one talks to their free weights. In walking your dog, you develop a richer, deeper relationship with your dog," says veterinarian Marty Becker, co-author of *Fitness Unleashed! A Dog and Owner's Guide to Losing Weight and Gaining Health Together*. While he was working on this book, Becker decided to practice what he preached and walk his dogs more. The result was a 42-pound (19 kg) weight loss for him.

Health Benefits

Losing weight is at least as important for your dog as it is for you. Slender dogs live almost 2 years longer than dogs who are just a little bit overweight. Slender dogs have less health problems, too. Arthritis, diabetes, and other diseases that are caused or made worse by extra pounds can truly reduce your dog's quality of life.

Just because your dog looks perfect to you doesn't mean that he's trim. In fact, we're more likely to be in denial about our dog's weight than our own. Almost half the owners of overweight pets who participated in the Northwestern University study described their pudgy dogs' condition as "ideal."

You and your dog might both have a slow metabolism. As much as 70 percent of the risk factor for obesity in dogs can be traced to your dog's breed, according to Becker. Greyhounds and Whippets almost all stay naturally lean, while stocky breeds like Pugs and Beagles tend to pack on the pounds. (This is an interesting point to ponder for those of us who are built more like Pugs than Greyhounds.) Still, with the right diet and exercise, dogs of all breeds can weigh the appropriate amount for their builds.

As for Pogo and me, we're doing great. I still have a way to go to get to my goal, but it's a lot closer than it was 11 months ago. I feel fabulous. Pogo is slender and, with all his added exercise, he gets to eat more than he did before his diet started. He's a happy boy.

If you and your dog need to shed some weight, or if you just want to stay in shape, it's fun to share in a healthy program of diet and fitness. So, snap on the leash and go for a walk, or find another type of exercise you both enjoy. It's the road to a great life for both of you. Pogo and I will see you out there.

Diet and fitness can help you both feel great!

Getting Competitive:

Chapter 8

Organized Sports and Activities

You just might find that, after you've played Living Room Agility or taught your dog to follow your scent trail around a couple of turns, you and your dog are hooked. You want the real deal!

Welcome to the subculture of people who have found *Dog*. We spend our weekends at trials, tournaments, and shows for our particular dog sport. We become friends and confidants. We have a great time. My favorite people in the world are those who have a passion for something. The world of dog sports is full of that kind of people.

Here are just a few organized sports and competitions that you and your little guy might want to get involved in.

Agility

In agility competition, dogs run through an obstacles course with hurdles, above-ground tunnels, weave poles, elevated dog walks (think balance beams for dogs), and A-frames (little Mount Everests!). Winning is based on accuracy and time, so the top dogs flash through the course. Competition is segregated by height, so little dogs have the same chance of winning as the big guys.

Show dogs must match their breed's standard as closely as possible.

Agility has become a huge spectator favorite. You can see competitions frequently aired on Animal Planet. An international competition also is held in this fast-paced sport. Who knows? It could end up an Olympic event some day.

In addition to the AKC, several other organizations offer agility. Check out the United States Agility Association (USDAA) at www.usdaa.com, the North American Dog Agility Council (NADAC) at www.nadac.com, and the United Kennel Club (UKC) at www.ukcdogs.com.

Conformation (Showing)

When you see the Westminster Kennel Club dog show on television, you're watching conformation competition. This is a little bit like a beauty contest, except the short, round-faced girl (the Pug) has just as much chance of winning as the tall, thin glamour girl with the long blonde hair (the Afghan Hound). Every breed has a written standard that describes the perfect specimen from nose to toes to tail, and the dog who comes closest to this blueprint for perfection (within its breed) wins.

Dogs who win in conformation competition come from breeders who carefully breed to the standard, so spend time at shows and get to understand the sport before buying a show dog.

To find upcoming dog shows in your area, go to www.akc.org and click on "Events."

Flyball

Flyball is extreme sport for dogs. The competitors race over a series of four hurdles and slap a box with their paws. The box spits out a tennis ball (little, tiny tennis balls for little, tiny dogs), the dogs snatch their balls mid-air, and race back over the hurdles. This is a relay race, with four dogs on each team. The fastest team wins.

Special interest surrounds little dogs in flyball competition. The height of the hurdles for each team is determined by the size of the shortest dog on the team. Every flyball team wants a short, speedy "height dog" who allows them to race with lower hurdle heights!

In competitive obedience, dogs retrieve dumbbells.

For more information, go to the North American Flyball Association at www.flyball.org.

Obedience

Competitive obedience is a lot more fun than it sounds. Yes, dogs Sit, Heel, and Come—but they also retrieve dumbbells over high jumps, find items just by scent, work on hand signals, and line up with all the strange dogs entered in the competition and do a 3-minute Sit-Stay and a 5-minute Down-Stay— while their owners leave the building. Little dogs can win every title the taller dogs can—and they look so cute while they're doing it!

For information, go to www.akc.org, click on "Events."

Rally-O

Rally-O is a bit of a mutt—a cross between competitive obedience and agility. This is a great starting place for new competitors (and their inexperienced dogs). Rally Obedience is something like a rally road race for sports cars. You and your dog negotiate through a series of exercises that vary each time. They include circling, heeling backward, weaving, and going over small hurdles. Dogs and humans love this new sport!

Ties are broken by the fastest time, so you and your little dog will want to

Little dogs can track scents just as well as the big guys.

beat feet to get the ribbons over the long-legged dogs.

For information go to www.akc.org, click on "Events."

Tracking

Your little dog's nose is just as magical as a big guys'. In AKC tracking events, dogs trail the scent of a human. This is a pass–fail event: The dog finds the items a human left behind, or he doesn't. Little dogs can do this work just as well as big dogs. It all depends on their wonderful, tiny noses.

For information, go to www.akc.org, click on "Events."

Trying New Things

I am only half-joking when I tell people I want to find a civil rights lawyer and sue dog clubs for discriminating against my dogs based on their Breed of Origin. Some sports are limited to certain breeds, even if breeds also are great at those sports.

For example, only breeds in the Herding Group (and a few other breeds with herding in their ancestry) can earn titles in any of the organizations that put on herding trials. Terriers and Dachshunds are the only breeds who can earn earthdog (ratting) titles.

My little Radar is a fabulous herder and a wonderful ratter. Because these tests are supposed to measure instinct and skills, it seems wrong to exclude a dog like Radar just because he's a Papillon. Let's face it, in the real world, it's not like someone would turn to Radar and say, "Oh no! Don't get that mouse! We have to wait for a terrier to arrive!"

Although titles are restricted in these sports, they are absolutely great fun to dabble in. In my experience, the people who actually do these sports welcome those of us with non-traditional breeds with open arms.

So, if you have the chance and a dog who likes to expand his abilities beyond what you might expect of a little dog, check out the following activities.

Earthdog

If other sports are a subculture, earthdog is a cult. These tests are intended to replicate a terrier going to quarry through underground tunnels. The participants build mounds of earth over wooden tunnels that have false turns and obstacles. At the end of the maze is a rat. (Don't worry—the rats are safely in cages. The dogs can't hurt the rats, and the rats can't hurt the dogs.)

Dogs who have the instinct to "go to ground" love it! When I went to an earthdog trial, they even let Radar run the course (after the dogs in the competition had completed their event). Radar would have nailed it!

For more information, go to the AKC website www.akc.org and click on "Events" to learn more about earthdog trials.

Herding

Herding dog trials are strictly limited to those few breeds that were originally bred to herd sheep and cattle. The only little dogs allowed in the competition are Corgis and Shelties. Some competition is limited to only Border Collies.

Still, it's worth it to go watch these wonderful dogs work. My favorite are the open-field Border Collie trials, in which these dogs run hundreds of yards to a small flock of sheep and take them through a rigorous course, maneuvering them through gates, separating one from the rest, and eventually

Radar herding ducks.

herding them into a small pen.

Some herding competition also includes ducks (that naturally flock, like sheep) and cattle.

Okay, it's a stretch for little dogs to share a sentence with the words "Border Collie." Still, some little dogs love to herd. If you want to learn more about herding, and maybe even find a place that will let you practice on ducks, a good website is the American Border Collie Network

Canine Freestyle (Dancing With Dogs)

Little dogs love to dance! For information and training tips about the fun activity dancing with dogs, check out Chapter 3. The largest canine musical freestyle club is the World Canine Freestyle Organization at www.worldcaninefreestyle.org.

at www.abcollie.com. They have a list of upcoming Border Collie competitions around the country and an archive of websites.

Two words of caution: I've taken my Radar herding several times (he *loves* it!), and I've had people tell me I should let him herd sheep. I think they are crazy. Do I think he could do it? Yes. However, Radar weighs 8 pounds (3.6 kg). Even big dogs are occasionally seriously injured by a sheep's hoof, or a rock that those hoofs send flying. Why would I expose my dog to any danger when he gets all the thrill of herding by moving ducks around?

The other caution is that many, even most, herding instructors can be rather heavy-handed on dogs. You can understand it: It's important that big, high-prey-drive dogs don't hurt the sheep they're supposed to be moving from place to place. However, for our little dogs, this is just a fun day. Don't spoil it by allowing anyone to scream at or throw a stick near your dog.

This is just a game for our guys!

Getting Started

It can be confusing for a beginner to get started. After all, the yellow pages are full of dog training schools, but chances are you don't see any listing for flyball or tracking.

The best bet is go see the people who are actually doing your sport. Bring a chair or plant yourself on the bleachers, and observe. Who is successful at the sport? More important, who's got a relationship with their dog that you admire?

When There Isn't a Great Local Class

You might be surprised how many classes exist in your sport, once you start getting to know the people in the hobby. Often, these specialized classes aren't listed in the yellow pages, because the best network is word-of-mouth among the people in the sport.

However, if no one is teaching in your area (or if no one is teaching your sport in a way that you admire), don't worry. Make arrangements to travel once a month to someone who's good in the sport, and take a private lesson.

Most sports have seminars around the country. They're a great place to learn techniques and make friends with other enthusiasts.

Is anyone competing using your breed, or at least another small-dog breed?

When the competitors aren't busy, talk to them. (Trust me, in every dog sport plenty of time is spent waiting, and most people are glad to answer polite questions.) Ask for their recommendations about how to get started in the sport in your area. These people can steer you to the right trainers and the local clubs for your sport.

Finding an Event

Sometimes, it's hard to find an event to observe! Happily, that's become much easier during recent years thanks to the Internet. If you do a search for your sport, chances are you'll find some websites that will lead you to some information.

The AKC is the largest dog registry in the United States, and it holds the most events. Go to www.akc.org and click on "Events." You can spend days just scrolling around. All upcoming events are listed on their website by state, and events are held all over the country. This is a great place to get started!

Selecting an Instructor

If you decide to pursue any of the dog sports in this book, chances are you're going to end up taking classes. Dog training is a visual, tactile process that's all about timing, and nothing replaces a great class. On the other hand, nothing does more damage than a bad class. A bad experience can sour you to a sport, teach you bad habits instead of good ones, and damage the relationship you have with your dog.

Competition and Your Dog

Humans are competitive by nature. We've taken our ancient relationship with dogs and turned the things we do together into competitive events. That can be fun—but it can also be destructive to our relationships with our dogs. I've seen agility and competitive obedience dogs wilt under their owner's expectations. Don't spoil the fun for your dog by making him only think about the mistakes he might make.

Think about how you've felt when you were under too much pressure—and don't make your dog feel the same way. For me, it's an only-in-retrospect funny story of junior high gym class. I got stuck on the gymnastics horse in front of all the cute jocks. The more upset I got, the worse I struggled, and the more embarrassed I became. The moral: The more pressure you put on yourself and your dog, the worse you will be. If you decide to compete, relax and have fun. Don't worry about anyone else. Don't worry about ribbons and scores and titles.

Before I go into the ring with my dog, I always look down and say, "I'm so happy to be with you here today." I remember how lucky I am to be with my wonderful little buddy, doing something so amazing, with such an accomplished dog. I relax and enjoy the moment.

Don't ever put your dog under as much pressure as I put on myself in that long-ago gym class.

Go watch the classes in your area before you sign up. Ask the instruction questions. Here are some things to look for before you show up with your little dog at a class:

* Is the class safe for little dogs? Some of these sports, like agility and flyball, really rev up the dogs' prey drive. You must take your lessons from someone who keeps the dogs motivated, yet under control enough to be safe.

* Is the instructor knowledgeable about the sport? I'm constantly amazed at the classes that various people feel qualified to teach. For example, you should be taking competitive obedience classes from someone who has multiple Utility Dog titles, not someone who squeaked her way into a single Companion Dog title. If someone isn't successful at the sport herself, how can she teach it to you? I have seen instructors who teach such poor handling techniques to their students that the students have to spend years to unlearn what they were taught.

* Does the instructor use gentle methods? Gentle training methods are

important for all dogs—they are essential for small ones. Remember, even if you are kind to your dog in class, he will be worried if other people are jerking on choke chains and yelling at their dogs. If you get a queasy feeling in your stomach about a trainer's methods, go somewhere else. More choices are available than ever before.

❋ Has the instructor successfully competed with little dogs, or at least trained someone who has? The body cues and timing really are different when you have a small dog, and nothing beats that first-hand experience. However, small dogs are relatively rare in competitive events, so there aren't always trainers—especially trainers who communicate and teach a beginner well—who have personally competed with a little guy. If you find a trainer who has students who have successfully competed with little dogs, that's probably a great place to take a class.

❋ Are the dogs and humans having a good time with each other? Dog sports are supposed to intensify the bond we feel together, not damage it. Look for classes where people are smiling and talking with each other, and dogs are joyfully wagging their tails. If the people are tense and the dogs are stressed, think about it: Is that the way you want to spend you "fun" hours with your dog?

❋ Does the instructor have the ability to teach as well as train? Training a dog and teaching a human are two rare and unrelated skills. Dog training is a nonverbal experience that is hard to put into words. If you find someone who can translate that nonverbal experience into teachable moments, latch on to her! Appreciate the rare gift she has!

Keep training fun and interesting.

Hitting The Road:

Chapter 9

Traveling With Tiny Dogs

One of the great things  about portable-sized dogs is that they're—well—portable. It can be hard to bring a Saint Bernard or Great Dane along on vacation, but you can go just about anywhere with your toy-sized companion.

So, whether it's taking a little break in a busy day for a cappuccino with your Chihuahua, or boarding a plane with your Pomeranian and heading across the country, you can have a great time!

Around Town

Going out with your dog around town can be a fun experience for both of you.

Your Dog, Dinner, and Drinks

Give yourself a "mini-vacation" in your home town by bringing your dog with you when you stop for an espresso or go out to dinner.

Health laws generally prohibit dogs in a building where food is served, but an ever-growing number of restaurants, coffee houses, and even brew pubs have outdoor areas where pets are welcome. When the weather is good, go have some fun!

Invite a friend and his dog, if you want. (That's a great way to break ice for a friendly, low-key first date.) Or, just enjoy a table for two—you and your four-footed family member.

Dos and Don'ts of Doggie Dining

❋ Check ahead to make sure dogs are welcome. Just because state law allows dogs to eat al-fresco doesn't mean that restaurants must welcome them.

❋ Make sure your dog is comfortable. Ask for water for him if it's a warm day and you'll be there for a while.

❋ Don't let him bother others. You might love it when your dog licks your toes, but the people at the table next to you may not. This is a good time for your dog to sit in an unzipped purse-style carrier, so he's confined, but still talking with you.

❋ Leave a generous tip. You want the staff to welcome your dog—and other people's dogs—in the future.

❋ Don't sneak your dog into a restaurant where he isn't allowed. Worse yet, don't lie and say that your dog is a service dog (service dogs, such as guide dogs for the blind and seizure-alert dogs, are allowed in restaurants) if he's just your buddy. Yes, I agree with you that dogs should be allowed on general principle—but leaving an impression that your dog is a working service dog is like parking in a handicapped parking space. It's just wrong.

Your dog might enjoy a trip out to a canine-friendly restaurant.

Get your little dog used to traveling in a carrier.

Take Your Dog Shopping

You know that pet supply stores welcome dogs, but you might be surprised how many retail stores allow a dog—especially a small, well-behaved one. Your neighborhood "big-box" home improvement retailer probably allows dogs (most of them do). High-end, luxury retailers practically fawn over your dog. New York retailers Tiffany and Company and Bergdorf Goodman, among others, are pet-friendly.

So, go have some retail therapy and bring the one family member who knows enough not to say a word when you ask if a pair of pants makes your butt look big! And don't forget to buy the doggie some bling, while you're there.

By the way, don't forget the cardinal rule: Your dog pees on it, you buy it.

Dog Parks

Dog parks are a great way to meet other dog lovers in your area. Dog park people have an instant bond. And, if you are traveling, dog parks are a great way to learn about the city you're visiting. You can ask people for the best places to eat and the most interesting local sites. You'll get an insider's guide to the city, which is a lot more fun than any travel guide. It's all the advantages of having relatives in a city, but none of the disadvantages!

Use common sense in any dog park, especially since you have a smaller dog. Watch so that other dogs don't overwhelm him or decide to bully the newcomer. If your dog isn't a dog-park dog at home, he won't like them in other cities, either. But if you and your dog are happy and comfortable in dog parks, you'll love discovering the dog park culture in other cities!

Out-of-Town

Vacationing with your little dog is a snap. Think ahead and be prepared.

Flying with Your Dog

While the big dogs have to fly in cargo, the little dogs can ride in the cabin with you. However, you have to plan ahead of time to fly with your dog.

* **He needs to travel in an airline-approved carry-on bag.** Check the airline's website to be sure that the exact carrier you have is approved for that airline.

* **Expect to pay for your pup's flight.** Although you will be carrying your dog with you instead of a carry-on bag, airlines do charge a fee for this. The days are long gone when you might have been able to sneak a little dog on board (which wasn't ever a good idea anyway). With the airport security systems now in place, you and your dog will be grounded if you haven't paid.

* **Make reservations well in advance.** Airlines each have individual policies about how many dogs are allowed in the cabin. It can be as few as one or two for the entire plane. Make reservations early to make sure your dog has a place on the plane.

Getting Used to the Carrier

If you're going to travel together, your dog must be comfortable being schlepped around in a doggie carrier. If he's screeching, screaming, and shaking, or he's bent on jumping from the carrier, you'll never be able to carry him on a plane.

Teach your dog that his carrier is a great place to be. Make the bag like a drive-in restaurant for dog treats. Toss a treat in the bag, and let him run into the carrier and eat the treat. After he enjoys that, place him gently in the carrier and give him treats. Make a fuss over him. Tell him how handsome he looks.

Every time you place him in the carrier, give him a special word so that he knows what to expect. So, say "Carrier!" and then gently place

Hi There!

Did you know that people are three times more likely to talk with someone who is walking a dog than talk to someone who is alone? If you're traveling alone, having your dog with you will make your trip more interactive with people.

him in the bag and fuss and treat.

Don't zip up the carrier until he likes sitting in it unzipped. Once he's learned that a zipped carrier has treats, then walk around your house with him, again telling him just how cool and fun this is. Then give him more treats.

Take him for some car rides in his bag, ending up at fun destinations such as a park or his favorite pet store to buy a toy. Spend some time doing this now, and you'll have a dog who leaps joyfully into his carriers for a lifetime.

Fly by Cargo? No Thanks!

Small-dog owners are very lucky, because our dogs can come on the plane with us. It is much safer than flying by cargo. While the airlines usually deliver

If you are flying with your dog, make sure the carrier is airline-approved.

the pets safe and sound, rarely, things can go wrong. Just think of the sad story of Vivi the Whippet who was flying home after the Westminster Kennel Club dog show in 2006. Somehow, Vivi got out of her crate, bolted from the area, and was lost in the vast expanses of the airport.

Because we can carry our dogs with us, we should. I would use cargo only in case of an absolute emergency. And, if my dog were in cargo, I'd certainly consider a GlobalPetFinder (see box) to add a little more security to my dog's trip.

Where to Stay

Most hotels and motels accept a well-behaved small dog. Whether you're an economy sleeper or a luxury napper, you can find plenty of choices in your price range. The national Motel 6 chain advertises its pet-friendly policies, and you should see what the Ritz Carlton in New York does for its four-footed guests.

Do ask about extra nightly charges. A fee per dog per night usually is charged, and this fee may not be refundable even if your dog is perfectly behaved.

Several books and websites list pet-friendly hotel information, like www.petswelcome.com. They boast that they have complete listings for 25,000 pet-friendly hotels, B&Bs, ski resorts, campgrounds, and beaches.

Hotel Petiquette

* Don't leave the dog alone in the room (hire a sitter if you need to).
* Keep him confined to make sure no accidents occur. You don't want the next person who checks in to find dog pee on the corner of the bedspread.
* Don't let your dog bark. They're naturally more vigilant when you're away, so they tend to be particularly "verbally gifted" if you don't supervise them carefully.

Call ahead to check if your hotel accepts dogs.

Putting on the Ritz

If you want to check out the ultimate in canine comfort, check out the V.I.P. ("Very Important Pooch") program that the Ritz-Carlton in New York introduced a few years ago. This program allows dogs to enjoy the use of ultra-chic pet carriers, 22-karat gold-plated identification tags, aromatherapy coat spritz treatments, home-baked dog treats and carob "bon-bons," ceramic dinnerware, bone-shaped plush stuffed doggy pillows, and luxury quilted travel mats. In case a canine guest should forget to pack appropriately for the unpredictable New York City weather, rainproof trench coats, leather jackets, and cashmere sweaters are on loan at the hotel's concierge desk.

For a few bones, your dog could upgrade to the Doggy & Me Package, which includes:
- Overnight luxury accommodations for two in a Superior Guestroom
- Gift certificate to be used toward purchases from the Jazzy Couture Collection for pets at Saks Fifth Avenue
- Portrait of Very Important Pooch and their master in Central Park by Jeff Moore, pet photographer
- Basket of gourmet treats for the Very Important Pooch,  including doggy pizzas and black-and-white cookies (may be decorated with the dog's name upon request)

Anything else your dog wants, the hotel staff will find. "There is no request that is too small," said a hotel spokesperson.

❋ Whenever you travel, there's an extra danger of losing your dog. I can't imagine what it would be like to lose a dog in a strange city. Be sure your dog has plenty of identification on him when you are traveling!

Tags

For the best protection, your dog should have both his license and a tag with your contact information. (You can get tags that you can personalize at any large "big-box" pet supply store, and they are widely available on-line.) Be sure the tags have a number that you can access during your vacation, so if someone calls you to say that they've found your pet, you can meet them. Tags are the best bet for a safe, happy, and speedy reunion with your prodigal pooch.

Microchips

A microchip is a rice-sized computer chip that's injected into your dog at the veterinarian's office. The chip has a unique number that allows the company that issued the chip to find you. Almost all veterinary offices and animal shelters have scanners that read chips. Collars can come off, and some bad guys will even take off the collar of a lost or stolen dog. Microchips are forever.

Global Positioning System

Keep your dog identified with tags on his collar.

The big news in finding lost pets is the GlobalPetFinder (www.globalpetfinder.com), a global positioning system for your dog. The device attaches to your dog's collar. Think of it as OnStar for canines.

This relatively new device sends updates of your pet's location to your cell phone and computer, tracking his whereabouts. At the time of writing, the device available was too large for small dogs (the manufacturer recommends it for dogs over 30 pounds [13.6 kg]). However, a version small enough for dogs as little as 8 pounds (3.6 kg) is scheduled to become available soon.

Here's the verdict:

❋ The device works better in a city than in the country. It tracks the dog's location to within about 50 feet of a city address. However, for wilderness areas where no street addresses are available, the device gives a reading of how far the dog is (and in which direction) from a fixed point, such as your home. It narrows down the search area much better in the city than the country.

* It's expensive. The device itself is costly, and a lot of fees are associated with use—an activation fee, plus monthly fees that require a year's subscription to the service. The battery life is only 1 to 5 days, so it's important to have an extra set of the rechargeable batteries and to replace them regularly.
* Given the costs and the limitations, this device has limited uses. But a long road trip, during which dogs can become disoriented and bored, might be one of those uses.
* If an emergency situation occurs that required my dog to travel in a plane in cargo, I would certainly put a harness on him and attach the device.

You're not alone when you're traveling with your dog. Stay safe, mind your "petiquette," and both of you will enjoy getting out of the house and having new adventures, whether it's at the local coffee shop or a real-life French bistro.

Good planning will help ensure a safe and fun trip.

A Joyful Gift:

Chapter 10

Becoming a Therapy Dog

When my car gets near the hospital, my Papillon, Pogo, starts whining and scratching at his crate. He can't wait to get out. He reminds me of a Border Collie who knows he's about to herd sheep. Pogo is excited because he's about to go on a therapy visit to a children's hospital. There's nothing that he loves better.

If you have a dog who likes people and likes being touched, volunteering as a therapy dog team might be the best thing that ever happened to you. We choose to visit a children's hospital because Pogo absolutely adores children, but countless other places need the warmth, love, and healing abilities of dogs. They include nursing homes and residential care facilities, hospices, schools, libraries—the list extends to any place where people will feel better if a loving dog comes to visit and pay attention to them.

A place exists for all kinds of therapy dogs (and even therapy cats, bunnies, miniature horses, llamas, and other creatures)—every animal who does this work has his or her special gift. However, a special need exists for little therapy dogs. Some people are afraid of dogs, but it's almost impossible to be afraid of small dogs who tend to look more like stuffed

Must Love People and Petting

The most important trait of a potential therapy dog is that he loves people and enjoys their touch. If your dog has that type of personality, he can almost certainly be trained to pass the therapy dog requirements.

animals than dogs. Many people who receive therapy visits are confined to a bed—a little dog (with permission, of course) can sit on the bed and comfort and snuggle with them. Little dogs can fit on the laps of people in wheelchairs.

One other plus about small dogs—most toy breeds were created solely for companionship, making them naturals at sitting on laps, accepting attention, and generally being an all-around love sponge. Your little dog may be perfect for bringing a smile and support to people in need.

Therapy Organizations

Several organizations certify therapy dogs, including Therapy Dogs International, Delta Society, and Therapy Dogs, Inc. Each has a qualifying test that they've developed to screen for the kinds of skills that therapy dogs need.

Dogs who love children can make great therapy dogs.

Therapy Organizations

Delta Society
Pet Partners Program
875 124th Avenue NE, Suite101
Bellevue, WA 98005-2531
(425) 226-7357
www.deltasociety.org

Therapy Dogs International
88 Bartley Road
Flanders, NJ 07836
973-252-9800
www.tdi-dog.org

Therapy Dogs, Inc.
P.O. Box 5868
Cheyenne, WY 82003
877-843-7364
www.therapydogs.com

The tests are designed to make sure the dogs are well-behaved, welcome touch, and aren't rattled by unusual noises or odd behavior from people. The three major therapy organizations have certified over 20,000 animals to do this work.

What Therapy Organizations Provide

All the major organizations, and most of the minor ones, provide liability insurance for their volunteers. It's important to have that kind of coverage because you are likely visiting medically fragile people, and people whom you do not know. Most of the organizations offer liability coverage for therapy dog visits as part of their membership.

The organizations also provide support. They may help you find places to volunteer, provide mentoring, or have publications and conferences that give you ongoing training and support.

It's important to volunteer through one of the reputable nonprofit groups that are doing this work.

What It Takes

Your dog must pass a qualifying test. The Delta Society's Pet Partners Evaluation Process is a good example of what you and your dog need to accomplish as a team in a two-part test.

The first half of the test is the Pet Partners Skills Test, which is based on the AKC Canine Good Citizen (CGC) Test. This part of the test is designed to

Therapy dogs must be exposed to wheelchairs and medical equipment.

determine if the dog is under control and can follow basic commands. The dog has to accept petting; show that he follows basic commands such as Sit, Down, Stay, and Come; that he'll ignore another dog who comes near; and that he won't react fearfully or aggressively to a loud noise. He also must walk calmly on a loose leash through people coming by with medical equipment.

The second half of the evaluation is the Pet Partners Aptitude Test, which is designed to simulate conditions that the therapy team may encounter on a visit. The handler is expected to role-play, acting as if he or she is visiting a facility. This part of the test includes much more touching of the dog (including being petted by three people at once), clumsy petting, people who are making loud noises, interacting with people in wheelchairs and walkers, and leaving a toy alone when told not to touch it. The aptitude test is a series of scenarios that flow from one to another, becoming more demanding as the test progresses.

In addition to passing the evaluation, the team must also:

* Be well-groomed and appropriately dressed.
* Have a certificate from the dog's veterinarian that the dog is appropriate for this work
* Certify that the dog has never had aggression training
* Dogs with disabilities are very welcome in the Pet Partner program.

Each therapy organization has differing requirements, so check with them about their procedures.

Test Tip

If you have a very small dog (under about 10 pounds), you can choose to carry him in parts of the test. He will be tested on how well he sits on a person's lap and other special conditions for small dogs.

The AKC Canine Good Citizen (CGC) Test

The American Kennel Club's Good Citizen (CGC) Test evaluates practical, useful skills: walking politely on a loose leash; accepting petting and grooming; staying under control when another is dog near.

Any dog, with some training, has the ability to pass this practical test. Although it is administered through the AKC, dogs don't have to be purebred to earn the CGC designation.

The CGC test also is the basis for much of the evaluation of therapy dogs in each organization.

The CGC tests for these 10 skills:

1. Accepting a friendly stranger
2. Sitting politely for petting
3. Appearance and grooming
4. Out for a walk (walking on a loose lead).
5. Walking through a crowd
6. Sit and down on command and staying in place
7. Coming when called
8. Reaction to another dog.
9. Reaction to distraction
10. Supervised separation

Getting Started

Just as every human isn't cut out to be a social worker, not every dog is born to be a therapy dog. Here are the traits of dogs who will enjoy this work:

1. They like strangers. No one wants a therapy dog who doesn't like them!

2. They like being touched and held.

3. They're confident. You're asking your little dog to go to strange places full of stressed people. Hospitals have slippery floors, schools have loud bells, and every institution has its own smells. It takes a confident little dog to see these situations as fun.

If you're thinking about therapy work, be sure that your puppy is well-socialized (see Chapter 11). Introduce him to a wide variety of people, including people of different races, ethnic groups, and ages. Take him places that have wheelchairs, so he doesn't think they're scary or unusual.

Be sure that lots of people hold your little puppy, so he learns that each pair of new hands represents another fun time with a new friend.

If you're looking for a dog with the specific goal of doing therapy work, consider adopting an adult rescue dog. You'll know if the dog has the right personality to do

As a therapy dog, your dog can spread joy (and kisses)!

this work, and you'll offer a rescue the chance of a lifetime!

A Therapy Team

I cannot tell you how magical it is volunteering with Pogo in this work. In other things we do, I'm the leader and he's the follower. In this job, Pogo is the senior partner. I think of myself as his spotter: My job is to make sure he's safe and secure so he can do what he does best.

When Pogo arrives at the hospital, his personality transforms. If you've read other chapters in this book, you know that Pogo can be a high-octane kind of dog. He got a name like "Pogo" (as in pogo stick) for a reason!

When Pogo walks inside those doors, he takes all that energy and focuses it on healing. I believe with all my heart that he knows exactly what he is doing. Most of the time, at the hospital, he's in my arms, on a bed, or on someone's lap. He often reaches out his paw to touch people—the children, the hospital staff, the kids' parents.

He puts his paw on the exact same spot on people's arms at some point in almost every visit. He reaches out so deliberately and precisely, I asked my acupuncturist if an acupuncture point was located there. My acupuncturist looked startled. She told me, "That's the point for sorrow." I think my little dog is taking away the sorrow when he visits.

Pogo always senses what a child needs. If a child is very sick, or in pain, Pogo just lies very quietly next to the child, sometimes only touching with his fur. I've seen him lie still without moving for 20 minutes, just giving out his gentle energy.

Other times, Pogo knows it's time to make kids smile. I've seen him sit on a bed and make up games with a child. I've seen him sit patiently for a quarter-hour while a child made up stories about their adventures together (Pogo was the fairy step-dog in an absolutely wonderful fractured fairy tale one girl made up).

Pogo and Rachael

Not a week goes by that Pogo doesn't perform a miracle, large or small. This visit to a girl I'm calling Rachael (not her real name) showed me so much of what makes me want to participate in the therapy program.

We're called in every once in a while by the hospital's staff to help them work with an animal-loving child. We'd visited Rachael a few times before, and she was making slow but noticeable progress from some sort of brain injury. This day, the staff was trying to get Rachael to make a conscious sound, something she hadn't done since her injury.

Because she'd always been a big animal lover, the staff thought that Pogo could help reach in through the haze and help her communicate. Pogo was very different with Rachael that day. Rather than just lying passively next to her, he kept gently pawing at her, as if to say, "Hey, come on out!"

The speech therapist asked Pogo to sit on Rachael's lap. I showed him where to sit, but he clearly didn't want to do it. I've learned never to push Pogo. I said, "Pogo doesn't seem to think he's supposed to be on Rachael's lap." Rachael's mother, a devoted and kind woman, looked up and said, "You know, she always loved animals, but liked them next to her, not on her lap." Somehow, Pogo knew that.

Pogo sat himself up against her pillow, looking like he was relaxing in a recliner next to Rachael. The speech therapy session began.

"If you make a noise, Pogo will kiss you," the therapist told Rachael. I tried to get the therapist's attention. I'd never taught Pogo to kiss on command—and now she'd promised a kiss.

Before I could say anything, Rachael made a noise. It wasn't a sentence. It wasn't even a word. But it was the very first time that she'd shown she was capable of making a voluntary sound.

My little dog knew exactly what to do. Without a word from the therapist or from me, Pogo calmly and gently reached over and kissed Rachael's face.

He always knows what to do.

As we leave our "rounds" (which typically last somewhere between 1 and 3 hours, depending on the day), Pogo always looks at me and wags his tail. My cocky little dog is back to his usual self.

Think about how lucky someone would be to have your dog visit. You know that you have the very best dog in the world. This is a chance for other people to find that they think you're dog is the best in the world, too.

Part 3

Activities for the Young— And Young at Heart

Chapter 11

The Little Puppy's Activity Chapter

Puppies need to have fun, too!

Fun is serious business for your puppy. Just as play for human children is an important part of what prepares them for a successful life, puppy play help your dog become confident and happy with you, other people, and other dogs.

Part of proper play comes from proper socialization—which means training your dog to get along in society. Here's what we know: Puppies who have been socialized and handled grow up to be smarter than other dogs, less likely to get sick, and calmer than other animals. The activities described in this chapter are really learning opportunities in disguise! Follow them, and you'll be able to participate in just about any activity, sport, or fun time your dog is able to do.

The first year of your dog's life is a time that you can never get back. It's when dogs learn get along with other dogs, with people, and with new situations. Do it right, and you'll be rewarded every day of your dog's long and happy life.

The Socialization Timeline

The following are the crucial socialization periods in a puppy's life:

⚘ **1–2 weeks:** Daily brief periods of handling by breeder. Puppies learn

Have a Grown-Up Rescue Dog?

Not every dog (or human) gets a happy childhood. While it's ideal to expose a puppy to the things described in this chapter, don't give up on your older dog! You can use the same methods described in this chapter to take your adopted dog new places, expose him to new things, and let him meet new people. He will get more confident and more social if he's given a chance.

Of course, life is a lot easier when we start with a good foundation that builds our confidence. Still, for people or pooches, it's never too late to have a happy childhood!

human contact is a positive part of life.

* **2–3 weeks:** More extensive and frequent puppy handling by the breeder and close friends. Introduce toys, different flooring, normal noises of living. Puppies learn to deal with very mild stress.

* **4–12 weeks:** Dog play is serious business for puppies at this age. They learn etiquette from other puppies in litter, their mother, and other dogs in the household. (Puppies leaving their litters younger than about 8 weeks may have difficulty relating with other dogs.) Expose the puppy to people of both genders, all ages, and preferably a range of appearances. Introduce car rides, new noises, indoor and outdoor play areas, trips to new locations. A new owner must continue the socialization begun by the breeder.

* **12–16 weeks:** Teach house manners, go to puppy kindergarten to meet dogs of different breeds and different temperaments, increase exposure to a widening circle of people.

* **16 weeks–2 years:** Build on the good foundation. Classes, walks, play dates with other dogs, continued exposure to a wide variety of people. If early socialization lessons aren't reinforced, they will be forgotten.

A good breeder starts the socialization process early.

A Good Start

The best breeders expose their puppies to human touch from the first day they are born. They make sure the puppy meets kids, friends, and neighbors. Puppies who know that humans are a part of life simply like people better than those puppies who didn't get that chance.

The best breeders also make sure that, at the appropriate ages, their puppies are exposed to new situations. That starts with learning to walk on different surfaces, such as carpeting and tile floors. They'll be given a couple of car rides and learn that cars are just another great place. They'll play inside and out (unless it's Minnesota in winter). They'll play with their littermates, and get to know other adult dogs in the household.

Unless you've bred your own puppy, you can't control these precious weeks. What you can do is seek out a breeder who gives her puppies this kind of start in life.

But a great breeder is just the beginning. The real joy of introducing your puppy to the world is for you. Take the time to do this!

The Effects of Separation

Pat Hastings, author of *Another Piece of the Puzzle: Puppy Development*, is one of the nation's leading authorities on puppy development. She uses the story of a Doberman Pinscher who was separated too young from other dogs as a cautionary tale for dog owners.

This Doberman was born back before the parvovirus vaccine was developed. As happened all too often back then (even in the best of loving homes), this dog and his littermates contracted the deadly disease. The puppy was separated from other dogs from the time he was 4 weeks old until he was 8 weeks old.

Teach your puppy to walk on different surfaces.

The Dobie grew up to be a sweet, good-tempered dog who loved people. He had a career as a top-winning show dog. But he never had a single dog friend. "For the rest of his life, other dogs hated this dog," says Hastings. "They'd growl at him across the dog show grounds because he had no concept of dog body language."

Even the female dogs hated him. Top-winning show dogs like this one typically father a fair number of puppies, but not this one. The female Dobermans wouldn't let him near them!

When Should Puppy Come Home?

Puppies learn a lot from their moms and littermates. Behaviorists now universally agree that puppies taken away too early from their litters will have difficulties throughout their lifetimes communicating with other dogs.

Puppies should stay with their moms until they are *at least* 8 weeks old to really learn the ropes of doggie communication. *Small-breed puppies mature more slowly, and do best interacting with their moms and litters until they are 12 weeks old.*

That's why it's so important to handle a puppy's socialization period correctly.

What About Diseases and Germs?

Socializing your puppy is a balancing act. Until he's about 16 weeks old, he's still getting his puppy shots, which protect him against deadly diseases such as parvo and distemper. You obviously don't want to put his life in danger by exposing him to those diseases. On the other hand, if you wait until he's had all his puppy shots to let him meet people and other dogs, you've missed the best time for socialization.

The best advice is to go out there, but use caution.

Doggie diseases are most often carried through contact with sick dogs, or with their urine or feces. So, if you are in a park or a pet super store where there may have been unvaccinated or unhealthy dogs, don't put your puppy on the ground. We have little dogs, so hold yours in your arms!

Don't let him get in contact with strange dogs, especially those who obviously don't get the kind of care that a family pet should receive. Instead, visit friends who have healthy, well-cared for dogs so that your little guy can meet other dogs.

The Socialization Process

For the first couple of days after you bring your puppy home, give him a quiet time to get used to his new home and his new people. Then get your puppy show on the road! Here's how to get started socializing your puppy.

Meeting People

Your goal for the first 3 months is to introduce your puppy to at least five people a day. No kidding.

It's not hard. You can give your puppy a cue word that lets him know he's going to be meeting someone new. Every time my dogs see someone (or some creature) we're going to chat with, I always say, "Let's say hi." That's their cue that this is a safe, friendly human or dog, and they can relax.

Here are some ways to introduce your puppy to new people:

* Take your puppy to your favorite coffee spot, sit outside in the sun, and let people come up and "oooh" and "ahhh" over him.
* Go to your local mega pet-supply house, and browse with your pup.
* Check out the fashions at the doggie boutiques in town, with your puppy in tow.
* Many retailers welcome dogs in their stores. Go where your dog is welcome (and buy something to show those businesses that it pays to be pet-friendly).
* Have lunch with friends at an outside café that welcomes pets.
* Go to your veterinarian's office on a day when you aren't scheduled for shots— just so he gets petted and hugged and given treats by the people there.
* Go to a pet-friendly bookstore

Your puppy should be introduced to gentle, respectful children.

and browse in the dog section.

* Go to your neighborhood park.
* You get the idea. Anyplace you are allowed to bring a puppy—do it. He needs to meet people.

Are you a shy person? Well, dogs give us a chance to move outside our comfort zone. Besides, do you really think that anyone is paying attention to you when you have the world's cutest puppy on your lap? I don't think so! Just relax and give your puppy the chance to be an extrovert.

Do you live a bazillion miles away from the city? Rural areas have feed stores and nurseries to visit. Heck, nowadays they have coffee shops. Find where the people in your community congregate, and go there.

Make It Totally Positive

There's a little detail that you might not have heard when people advise you to socialize your puppy: These interactions must be entirely, absolutely, fabulously positive. *If a puppy has bad experiences when he's being socialized, he will learn the lesson that people are bad and scary—not good and kind!*

So, make sure he meets kids, but be sure they're kind and gentle children. Ask other people to hold him, but make sure they're appropriate for your little dog. Give him treats and praise and love and snuggles.

Sometimes, it can be a little embarrassing to tell someone that they can't hold your puppy. I always tell myself that, while other people might have bought their dogs for protection, my little dogs bought *me* for protection. It's my job to make sure my dogs aren't hurt or frightened by someone, no matter how well-meaning that person may be. As tactfully as I can, it's important for me to get my dog away from any situation I don't think is ideal for him.

Keep the sessions short. You want to go plenty of places, but you don't want to exhaust your little guy. He's not learning

Viva La Difference

It's important to introduce your dog to lots of different people, so he knows that his best buddies come in all sizes, shapes, and skin tones. Those new buddies might talk in a strange-sounding language, look different from you, or use a wheelchair. Those superficial differences soon won't matter to your dog: It's all good!

Reward your dog after he meets new people.

anything new when he's zonked out in a strange place, wondering if he'll ever go home. Still, puppies are designed to be social. Have a little common sense and a bit of empathy for your little guy, and you'll do just great.

Meeting Other Dogs

Little dogs are in big danger from other dogs on the street. A tussle between two big dogs is usually not going to cause anybody any real harm, but that same tussle between a big dog and one of our little guys, and our little dog could be grievously wounded.

The best protection for little dogs is to be socialized when they are young, so they know the language of communicating with other dogs. "Only dogs can teach puppies how to behave with other dogs," says Pat Hastings, one of the nation's leading authorities on puppy development. Your puppy must meet appropriate adult dogs and other puppies. That can be very hard to do when you have a delicate little toy-sized breed.

Finding Adult Dogs

Ideally, your puppy should be playing with small-sized adult dogs who can

Teach Your Puppy to Enjoy Being Touched All Over

Imagine how scary it must be for a little-breed puppy. After all, compared to your little guy, a human being is the size of a skyscraper!

One way to help your small-dog adjust to this big world is to get him used to being held and touched all over while he is a puppy. The best way is by always using the same words to let him know what's happening. For example, when I'm picking up a dog, I always say, "Lift up," and then pick him up securely.

I touch a puppy all over several times a day, teaching him the names of his body parts. So, when you touch your dog, give him treats as you say "Good nose!" or "Good feet!" Over time, he'll associate being touched—even in delicate areas—with a happy experience.

Teach him names for his eyes, ears, feet, nose, tail, teeth, tummy, and rear end.

Always make this touching fun. It's a happy time between the two of you. Ask other people to touch your dog as well, and have that person give your dog the treat.

show him the ropes. If you don't have adult dogs in your own home, you'll have to find a couple of them to safely introduce to your puppy. Your breeder might be able to suggest someone who has one of her dogs that's all grown up. You might meet nice little-sized dogs at a local pet boutique. A near-by doggie day care might be able to hook you up with a puppy-loving, appropriately sized adult dog.

Don't neglect introducing your little puppy to nice full-sized dogs, too. A good place to find a sweet, gentle, full-sized dog might be through your instructor at puppy kindergarten (see below for more on puppy kindergarten).

The Introduction

Always use good sense when introducing your puppy to other dogs. Ask if the other dog would like to meet your puppy (not all older dogs like puppies, just as not all older humans like small children). Have both dogs on a loose leash. Let them say "Hi"—sniffing rear ends and wagging tails. It's fine for these interactions to be brief.

If the dogs initiate some play—great. If the play turns rowdy, either separate the dogs or take them to a secure room or fenced area, and remove their leashes so they don't get tangled.

Remember to be calm—you don't want to signal to your puppy that he should be afraid of other dogs. At the same time, keep a sharp eye on the strange dog, especially if he's a large one. If he growls or his body becomes tense, take your dog out of the situation. Even friendly dogs with big feet can hurt your pint-sized pooch, so don't let play get too boisterous with a large dog.

Introducing Things

To introduce new things to your puppy, give him a cue that it's okay to interact with the foreign object. For objects, I teach "Check it out!" When the puppy touches or looks at the item, say "Good check it out!" and give the puppy a treat. If the dog finds something scary, find the closest distance he's comfortable from the scary item. So, if he's afraid of an umbrella, go to the distance where he's calm, and treat and reward the calm behavior. Then, get a few inches closer, and treat him when he relaxes. Never overdo it. If something worries a puppy, short, repeated, happy exposures just at the edge of his comfort zone are much better than forcing him near something that scares him.

Here's a partial list of people, animals, and things to expose your puppy to:

* A skateboard
* People of different races

Supervise introductions between dogs.

* People who speak in foreign languages (the pitch and pace of words can be noticeably different to a dog)
* People on bicycles
* People in wheelchairs
* People who use walkers
* Umbrellas
* Young children
* Big dogs
* Little dogs
* People with noisy shoes
* People cheering
* Loudspeakers
* People with sunglasses
* People in long, flapping coats or dresses
* Things that drop (but don't land on the puppy!)
* Metal clanging
* Gum popping
* Cats
* Other creatures, such as ferrets and rabbits
* Birds that talk
* Horses
* People wearing costumes
* People wearing hats

The Super Dogs

The Army slogan "Be all you can be" can apply to your little dog, too!

Testing of military puppies that were given slight amounts of stress (such as being held in certain ways for seconds a day) during the first 16 days of life proved these dogs had healthier immune systems and dealt better with stress than puppies who didn't get this stimulation. These puppies were dubbed "super dogs."

Your well-socialized puppy will grow up to be a healthier, happier, more confident dog, just like the super puppies do.

Puppy Kindergarten

Your dog's puppy kindergarten class may be one of the most important classes you ever take. A study of dogs rescued from a large shelter determined that the number-one factor in successful adoptions was puppy kindergarten. Other factors included how often the owners handled their puppies and how well the dogs responded to commands, which are also skills dogs learn in puppy school. The bottom line: Early education is a good investment!

A good puppy kindergarten will teach your dog basic obedience skills and the art of getting along with his puppy peers. The problem is that a bad puppy kindergarten class will make your puppy afraid of other dogs—and may even result in an injury. Choose your school carefully!

Puppies are usually welcome in puppy kindergarten at age 12 weeks. Before you commit to a class, go take a look. Is the instructor kind and patient with the little guys? After all, a puppy can learn commands like "Sit" "Lie down," and "Come," but he has the attention span of a gnat at this age! Training for puppies should be 100 percent gentle and positive. *Absolutely no choke collars or force should be used on a small-breed puppy!*

The hallmark of puppy kindergarten is the playtime among the puppies. Watch these group interactions like a hawk. Playtime is a free-for-all in far too many classes, where large-breed puppies mash small ones, and bullies run the class. This will teach your little guy to be terrified of other dogs, and it may even get him injured.

Puppies can get rambunctious, so choose your puppy kindergarten carefully.

Pogo and the Mastiff

When my dog Pogo was a youngster, I worried about him. He was too bold and thought he was too tough. At age 5 months, he'd really only spent a lot of time with other Papillons, and he clearly thought he was the toughest, strongest, coolest dude anyone was going to meet. That attitude can get a little dog in serious trouble. He'd developed the habit of barking at big dogs, something I was not pleased with.

Then Pogo had an experience that changed his life, thanks to a wonderful Mastiff named Sarge. Sarge was a gentle dog who happened to live with a bevy of Pomeranians—he was also a champion show dog and an advanced obedience dog. Even though his paws were the size of dinner plates and his head the size of a suitcase, he was sweet, perfectly behaved, and totally reliable. This was the perfect dog to have Pogo meet, up close and personal.

As soon as Pogo realized the sheer size of the dog he was greeting, his cocky attitude changed. The encounter, which lasted only a couple of minutes, changed Pogo's life in positive and profound ways. He never again barked a challenge at a big dog—he learned he wasn't the biggest, toughest dog on the planet.

But he learned this lesson with a gentle, sweet dog with a huge heart. Sarge never growled. He never made Pogo feel afraid. In fact, he made Pogo feel it's a good idea to be a buddy with a big guy.

Pogo is a therapy dog now. We sometimes visit sick kids with friends of ours who have big Newfoundlands and Bouviers des Flandres. The big dogs take the kids for rides, and Pogo rides on the carts with the kids. He's great buddies with the big dogs—he loves to hang out with them.

I often think of Sarge and what he did for my Pogo—and what that's allowed Pogo to do in his life. If I could have one wish, it would be for every puppy to have a dog like Sarge to show him how life is lived.

Look instead for someone who has puppies playing two or three at a time, and who carefully matches puppies for size, age, and temperament in their play. Those classes exist; you just have to find them.

If you don't find a good puppy kindergarten in your area, you might want to create your own play day. It's fun! Check out Chapter 6 for more information.

Fear Periods and Shy Puppies

Fear periods: Kids go through them. Puppies go through them.

Your puppy will be friendly and happy one day, and the next morning he'll be pulling back into your arms when you take him out for your morning latte. Don't worry; this is normal. This is just like the friendly little kid who's suddenly hiding behind mom's skirt.

While some puppies go through periods of fear, others are genetically shy, just like some people are shy. If your puppy is in a shy stage (or a shy lifetime), continue to socialize your puppy. If you leave your puppy at home, he'll never learn to cope. On the other hand, don't push your puppy too hard.

Many puppies go through a fear period.

"The way you get over a fear of spiders isn't by going into a room with 50,000 spiders," points out Tanya Roberts, director of behavior and training for the Oregon Humane Society. Pushing your poor little shy-phase puppy into a noisy, crowded place is the equivalent of that room full of spiders.

If your puppy is worried, make him feel safe and happy. Talk to him. Give him treats. Figure out how far away you need to be from what worries him for him to relax, and then, with treats, happy words, and body language, gradually work toward what worries him. When his body language tells you he's worried, back off; then work gradually forward.

He'll learn to trust you and to cope with his fears.

Golden Years and Good Times:

Chapter 12

Activities for Senior and Disabled Dogs

Puppies get lots of attention. There's puppy kindergarten, training for puppies, and dozens and dozens of books about how to help puppies grow up happy and strong.

What about the other end of our wonderful dog's lives? Older dogs (and dogs with debilitating physical conditions) need special attention, too.

It's heartbreaking to see our dogs age. What's even more frustrating is seeing a dog who still wants to do activities, but has an injury or illness that limits what he can do. This chapter is for those dogs, suggesting activities just for them. It will also give you some helpful resources, and even give you ways to adapt past activities to make your dog's life fun now.

Let's get started making those golden years truly golden!

When the Spirit Is Willing but the Flesh Is Weak

My dog Radar has always been an active guy. He's the one who will try anything with me: competitive obedience, flyball, herding, earthdog, and tracking. My Radar has been the ultimate "can do" dog.

Then his body started having serious problems. Two years ago, he was diagnosed with inflammatory bowel disease, a condition a lot like Crohn's disease in humans. We're lucky: So far, he's responded well to treatment,

Your dog's sense of smell won't decline in his later years.

and his prognosis looks very good for a long life.

But things will never be as they once were. Radar certainly doesn't have the stamina he once did. Some days, he just doesn't feel very well. And when he's feeling stressed, he shuts down. Currently, we take a Dancing with Dogs class, which allows us to choose movements that work for his body now.

You may have a dog like Radar, who still very much wants to use his clever brain. He wants his share of your time and attention, as he always had. Here are some activities that will allow you to make your dog's life just as rich and exciting as it ever was, while saving on the wear and tear that his body can no longer take.

Think About Your Dog's Needs

Think about your dog's limitations, but also take his abilities into account. Come up with ways to communicate what you need or to modify an activity for your dog.

* **Deaf dogs** need everything to be visual. You can "clicker train" a deaf dog with a bright light—flash the light when he's right rather than click! Make sure you have a "Good dog!" signal. Of course, all commands must be on hand signal. (A great resource for people with deaf dogs is the Deaf Dog Education Action Fund at www.deafdogs.org.)

* **Blind dogs** need guidance from you with words. Give them cues to help navigate their environments, such as "Step up" or "Step down." Caroline Levin has written books and made videos about training blind dogs. Go to www.petcarebooks.com to learn more.

* **Dogs with mobility problems,** such as arthritis or amputations, and **senior dogs** still want the same things other dogs do. Talk with your veterinarian about what your particular dog can—and can't—do. Is it okay for him to jump? How high? How far is it comfortable for him to walk? What activities make him lose his balance?

Make Your Dog Useful

Radar is my Useful Dog. He's the one I ask to pick up a pen when I drop it. He's the one I ask to go find Goldie when she's asleep in another room. He's the one who "helps" me cook (and scarfs up everything I drop on the floor). He's the dog I take to my dog-friendly bank when I deposit a check.

Think about what things your dog *can* do, rather than just what he can't, then ask him to do it. Be sure to tell your dog every day how much you appreciate him!

Take a look at the normal activities that dogs love, and adjust them according to your dog's needs. Then review the activities in this book, and select some that work for your dog's abilities.

All he cares about is that he's having fun with you!

Canine Brain Games

This book is full of tricks and games that are easy on the body but keep the brain busy. The Nose Games in Chapter 2 are mentally stimulating, and even tiring (in a good way). Even the oldest dog, who may have lost much of his sight and hearing, still retains his sense of smell.

Game #1: Which Hand?

Remember "Which Hand" in Chapter 2? Dogs of every single level of physical ability love this game. You put a treat in one hand and hold both fists out. When the dog picks the correct hand (which happens at least half the time!), he earns the reward.

For a deaf dog, holding out your hands becomes the signal to play the game.

Be sure the treats are good and smelly for the blind dog, and he'll figure it out in a heartbeat. If your dog has limited mobility, be sure to hold your hands in a way so that he can touch both.

This is an activity that even an injured dog on crate rest can participate in. It will help with that stir-crazy little guy who injured himself, and the veterinarian told you to keep him absolutely quiet for 6 weeks.

This incredibly simple game—and others you make up like it—can put you and your disabled dog back on the road to fun.

Game #2: The Shell Game

The Shell Game has the same kind of simple magic, because it relies entirely on your dog's undiminished sense of smell. Review the steps for playing "The Shell Game" in Chapter 2.

As in "Which Hand," make any adjustments needed for your dog. Create a hand signal for your deaf dog. Be sure your dog with limited mobility can easily reach the cup holding the treat with his nose or paw. This game is completely no-impact, and allows your dog to think and interact with you.

Game #3: Find-It and Tracking Games

The Find-It games in Chapter 2 teach your dog how to search for things by scent, including people, other animals, and your keys. Although these activities won't work for a dog who is completely immobile after surgery, they are low-impact. Find-It games can be played in the house; just make sure the hiding places are not too difficult to get to. They're great entertainment for a dog who has reduced mobility.

Game #4: Scent Tricks

The scent tricks in Chapter 5, including "Pick a Card" and "Flashcards," take a lot of concentration and thinking—and absolutely no physical exertion. If you have a dog who can play "Which Hand," teach your guy these games. These are complex behaviors and will do a lot to relieve the stress and boredom that disabled dogs experience.

Puzzle toys keep the mind occupied.

Use these tricks as a beginning. The more you train your dog, the more ideas will fall naturally into place. Remember to think about all the great things he *can* do— and give him the chance!

Take a Class

Dogs who must be completely immobilized as they recover from surgery or a traumatic injury can't take a class while their bodies are healing. However, many wonderful classes are available for dogs with chronic conditions or dogs who are a little farther along in the healing process from a traumatic injury.

Puzzle Toys

These toys (explained in detail in Chapter 4) engage the brain— toys that randomly release treats, or plush toys that the dog takes apart (and the human puts back together). A dog who is on crate rest—which means no walking, no jumping, no running, no playing—should have every single puzzle toy on the market! They are something that every dog with any disability can enjoy.

Almost all class instructors will be extremely sympathetic and helpful with your dog's condition. Explain the dog's limitations, and ask for help. Of course, never, ever do anything that doesn't feel right and safe to you. The idea is gentle fun, not how far you can push your little guy.

Dance Class

Canine Freestyle (see Chapter 3) is a great sport for dogs of all ages and all physical abilities, because you develop a routine that's appropriate for your dog and his abilities. My own Papillon Radar can't twist comfortably any more, so we don't use the "Twist" and "Spin" commands. However, he's absolutely fabulous at heeling and all kinds of circling patterns, so we incorporate those into our little routine.

Dogs with limited mobility can dance to a slow number. You can incorporate your hand signals into the routine for your deaf dog. A blind dog will require special attention, so make sure he feels safe and secure when and where you practice the routine.

Tricks Class

Lots of obedience schools have a tricks class. Like dance class, you can pick and choose which tricks work for your dog. Talk with the instructor before the

class, and see if you can have special accomm
odation for the needs of your dog. Your instructor
should know how to teach plenty of tricks that
match the learning abilities of your particular dog.

Modify tricks to match your dog's physical capabilities.

Modifying Other Classes

Sometimes, it's a matter of modifying and adapting
a class to fit your dog. For example, I know a three-
legged dog taking an agility class. This Australian
Shepherd is otherwise very healthy and active,
and has adjusted extremely well to his
disability. The owner of the dog met with
the instructor, and they figured
out which agility equipment
would be safe for the dog to use,
and what to avoid. They made
jumps 8 inches (20 cm) tall instead
of 20 inches (51 cm). With the
modifications, this dog gets real
exercise and the social reward of
being in a class.

One day, a child whose family
dog was in this agility class drew
pictures of the dogs. She drew the
Aussie with all four legs, because she hadn't noticed that he was
missing one!

Of course, not every disabled dog can do agility, but do think about what
your dog *can* do and what interests him, and then try to modify an activity so
he can do it.

Go Out (With a Little Equipment)

One of the worst aspects of being sick (for a human or a dog), is that you
never get out of the house. Nothing is more boring than seeing the same walls
every day. There's no reason not to take your dog for car rides, walks, and
even bike rides.

Go for a Drive

We're so busy telling a sick or injured dog "no" we forget to tell him "yes!" Take your little guy every where you can in the car with you. Even if it's just riding to the supermarket, have him tag along (just keep the errand short). Unless it's hot outside (or very cold), he'd rather be with you and stay in the car while you go places than be cooped up at home the whole time.

Of course, it's especially important that an injured or sick dog be kept safe in the car. Every dog should be in a crate when you drive, just as every child should be in a car seat and every adult should wear a seatbelt. No exceptions!

Go for a drive— but don't let your little dog behind the wheel!

Go for a Walk

Even if your dog can't walk the same distance he used to, maybe he can still walk a block. Keep going for walks, and give him every chance you can to keep his muscles as active and strong as possible. When he can't go farther, give him a lift. The ability to carry our dogs is one of the great advantages of having a little dog.

You can also use a pet stroller for walks. Pet strollers, now widely available, are a lot like a kid's stroller, but have mesh to keep the dog inside. Think of it as a crate on wheels, with a holder for your latte. With a stroller, your senior or disabled dog gets all the fresh air and sunshine of a walk. He still can bark at the birds, squirrels, and cats along the way. My Papillons, Goldie and Radar, both ride for part of our long walks in a stroller, and they love it. Goldie, especially, rides like the Queen of the Nile, pleased that she's being treated appropriately as I push her along!

Become a Therapy Dog

Therapy work isn't for every dog, and it certainly isn't for a dog who is sick or in pain.

However, some disabled dogs are among the best therapy dogs on the planet. If your dog has lost a leg to cancer, but is now healthy and ready for action, he might be a great volunteer in a children's cancer program. A deaf dog can relate to people with hearing difficulties. Think about it! Read more about therapy in Chapter 10.

Go for a Bike Ride

Biking with your senior or disabled dog is much easier these days. Chapter 7 explains all about trailers for the back of your bike, or a pet basket for the handlebars, in which your pet can safely and happily ride with you. If you get your dog outside, even as a passenger, he will be calmer, happier, and better able to cope with his limitations. You will be so glad you did.

Of course, introduce your dog to this activity gradually. It might be disorienting to a blind dog, so only do this with a dog who finds it fun. Most dogs will!

Eat Out

In nice weather, coffee shops and restaurants have outside tables. Many welcome well-behaved dogs. Take your old dog with you. You'll sip a latte, read the paper, visit with friends. This is what retirement is supposed to be like. For tips on eating out, check out Chapter 9.

Activities to Help Heal

Going out for rehab or alternative veterinary practices can not only keep your dog occupied, they can help with his quality of life.

Physical Rehab

Until recently very little could be offered to dogs with chronic pain. There weren't even any drugs available. Luckily for our dogs, things are so much better now.

The biggest news is the advent of physical rehabilitation for pets. Veterinarians (and some physical therapists) provide the same range of assistance given to

Little Red Wagon

If you don't want to invest in a pet stroller, a kid's wagon makes fine transportation, too. Just make sure your dog won't jump out!

people who need physical therapy. Underwater treadmills, electrical stimulation, whirlpools, range of motion exercises, and more are available.

The educational leader in this emerging profession is the University of Tennessee. For more information about what is available in the field, check out their rehab website at www.canineequinerehab.com.

Physical rehab might truly change your dog's life.

Try Some Alternatives

Alternative medicine may be an excellent choice for dealing with chronic pain. My dogs and I have found a lot of help for our aches and pains from acupuncture, chiropractic, and massage. And little Goldie's favorite activity every day is her Tellington Touch time with me.

Acupuncture

Acupuncture has been clinically proven to reduce chronic pain. People who haven't had acupuncture are always concerned about sticking needles into a dog. After all, that's got to hurt, right? Actually, it almost never hurts.

The kinds of needles that give you shots are thick, so they can deliver the vaccine into your body. Those needles hurt. Acupuncture needles are hair-thin and are designed to insert gently and painlessly into your skin. When you are getting acupuncture, many people (and presumably dogs) actually experience mild euphoria.

It's definitely one of those "can't hurt, might help" things to try!

Alternative medicine may be an excellent choice for dealing with chronic pain.

Make-Over!

Well, you don't need to color your dog's hair. But one of the things that happens with old dogs is that we tend to stop grooming them. We are so busy trying not to hurt them that they get just a little bit neglected.

With great care and gentleness, make sure you're keeping your old boy groomed. Trim his nails. Give him a bath in perfect, warm water with a great shampoo. Keep his teeth brushed.

Dogs always feel their best when they look great. You can just imagine your oldster looking in the mirror at his gray face and thinking, "You dog! You still got it!"

Many veterinarians now have specialized training in this technique. To find a veterinarian near you, go to The International Veterinary Acupuncture Society website (www.ivas.org). (You may also consider checking with a human acupuncturist in your area, if your state medical and veterinary laws allow acupuncturists to treat animals.)

Chiropractic

A chiropractic adjustment can also help hugely with chronic pain. If your animal is recovering from surgery or injury, he also may begin holding his body differently to compensate for the pain. If he's had an amputation, he will definitely hold his body differently. Chiropractic can help with the resulting problems.

The American Veterinary Chiropractic Association (www.animalchiropractic.org) provides training and certification for chiropractors and veterinarians. They have a list of certified practitioners on their website, which are split fairly evenly between the two professions. Members are in the United States, Canada, Europe, and Australia.

Massage

Massage has real physical benefits. Among other things, it promotes more rapid healing from injuries, improves blood circulation, stimulates the lymphatic system, and can even help manage chronic pain.

Professional massage therapists are beginning to offer massage services for your dog. In fact, some massage therapists will treat both you and your dog during a combined visit. (This just might be the perfect day with your dog.)

Some schools are now giving specialized courses to licensed massage therapists so that they can treat animals. One of those schools is the Northwest School of Animal Massage, which offers classes for both professionals and for people who want to learn more about massaging their own pets. Check them out at www.nwsam.com.

Remember to spend time together and enjoy each other.

Of course, you don't have to be a trained professional to give your dog the canine equivalent of a back rub. He needs and craves gentle touch. Help him feel good.

Tellington Touch (TTouch)

Developed by Linda Tellington-Jones, this is a gentle form of touch that promotes healing and calmness. My Goldie, who doesn't like petting, absolutely adores TTouch. She puts her little front paws on my lap, wags her tail, and clearly asks for that wonderful sensation.

Linda Tellington-Jones' website (www.tteam-ttouch.com) gives a listing of TTouch practitioners around the world, and also has books on the subject for sale.

Our older and disabled dogs have a special magic of their own. Sometimes, because their physical condition makes us sad, we unconsciously avoid petting them, fussing over them, and making them feel special.

The best activity you can do with your older dog is to sit down right now, shower him with affection, and tell him exactly how much you love him!

Now you know how to keep a dog who can't get around well entertained. How about some activities for humans who might be laid up? Maybe you're recovering from surgery, or are on bed rest, or just need to slow down a little bit. Here are some dog-themed puzzles to keep your mind occupied while your body is at rest. After your little guy is tired out from his day's activities, what could be more fun than trying your hand at these puzzles, with your little guy snoozing in your lap?

Dancing With Dogs Scramble Puzzle

Unscramble the words in the left-hand column. Then rearrange the letters in the yellow spaces to form three new words. A clue should be considered when finding the answer to the puzzle.

E D R E B

S W I T T

U F F Y L F

S O T E

The clue: Both the owner and the dancing dog had:

_ _ _   _ _ _ _   _ _ _ _

CLUE: Both the owner and the dancing dog had: TWO LEFT FEET

Solution: BREED TWIST FLUFFY TOES

Raindog Puzzle I

In this puzzle, the letters from above fall (like raindrops) to the squares directly below them, but must be rearranged. When you fill out the puzzle correctly, you'll have a clever quotation about dogs. (The author of the quotation is listed below the puzzle.)

Hints for solving: Look for single-letter words to start—those are always "A" or "I." Three-letter words are most often "THE" or "DOG."

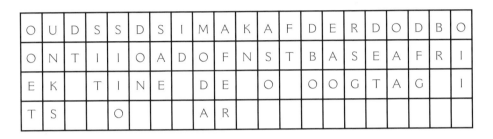

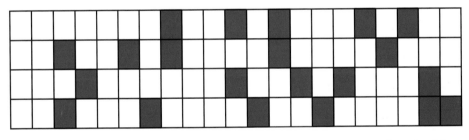

Groucho Marx

Sylla-Dog Puzzle

This puzzle separates the answers to the clues by syllable. From the syllables available, fill in the words. (The number of syllables in each word is in parentheses next to the space.) It's easiest if you cross off the syllables you use as you solve the puzzle.

When you read the first letters of the completed puzzle, they will spell out a clever saying about dogs.

SYLLABLES:

A · A · AF · AN · BET · CELL · CHI · DER · DOG · ENG · ENT · ER · ER · ER · EX · EX · FEN · FOUND · FRIEND · GIL · GREAT · HAUST · HUA · HUA · HUNT · I · I · I · I · IN · ING · ING · KE · LA · LAND · LISH · LY · MAL · MEG · NA · NA · NAUGHT · NEW · PEN · PER · PIN · O · O · O · RE · RI · RIN · RISH · ROTT · SCHER · SCHIP · STINCT · TAL · TER · TESE · TI · TIN · TIN · TRIEV · TY · UN · VER · VISZ · WEIL · Y

Clue	
The Lhasa Apso's country of origin	(2) — — — — —
The opposite of under	(2) — — — —
_____ Springer Spaniel	(2) — — — — — —
Famous German Shepherd of the 1950s	(3) — — — • — — — • — —
Large German dog breed—black with brown markings	(3) — — — — — — — — —
_____ Setter (red hunting dog)	(2) — — — — —
Small, black, Dutch dog in the Non-Sporting Group	(3) — — — — — — — —
Dog's first job with humans	(2) — — — — — —
"There's no need to fear, _____ is here" (old cartoon show with Wally Cox)	(3) — — — — — — —
All-white dog in the Toy Group	(2) — — — — — —
Rare dog in the Toy Group—known as the "mustachioed devil" —and the first dog alphabetically in the AKC	(4) — — — — — — — — — — — — —
Big black water dog from Canada	(3) — — — — — — — — — —
Scottish or West Highland White _____	(3) — — — — — — —
Opposite of Alpha	(3) — — — — —
Extroverted; likes people (a good trait in a therapy dog)	(2) — — — — — — —
Not closed	(2) — — — —
Labrador or Golden _____	(3) — — — — — — —
_____ Dane	(1) — — — —
_____ Greyhound (small sight hound in the Toy Group)	(4) — — — — — — —
Hungarian pointing dog	(2) — — — — —
Companion Dog _____ (advanced obedience title)	(3) — — — — — — — —

Smallest dog breed (from Mexico)   (3) — — —

Sport in which dogs run through an obstacle course   (4) — — — — — — —

Santa wants to know: Is your dog _____ or nice?   (2) — — — — — — —

An animal's natural behavior   (2) — — — — — — — —

The name of the dog in "Peter Pan"   (2) — — — —

Extremely tiring   (3) — — — — — — — — —

— —   — — —   — —   — — — — —   — —   — — — — — —   — — — — — —

TO ERR IS HUMAN, TO FORGIVE CANINE

Solution:

Clue	Answer
The Lhasa Apso's country of origin	TIBET (2)
The opposite of under	OVER (2)
Springer Spaniel _____	ENGLISH (2)
Famous German Shepherd of the 1950s (3 words)	RIN-TIN-TIN (3)
Large German dog breed—black with brown markings	ROTTWEILER (3)
Setter (red hunting dog) _____	IRISH (4)
Small, black, Dutch dog in the Non-Sporting Group	SCHIPPERKE (3)
Dog's first job with humans	HUNTING (2)
"There's no need to fear, _____ is here" (old cartoon show with Wally Cox)	UNDERDOG (3)
All-white dog in the Toy Group	MALTESE (2)
Rare dog in the Toy Group—known as the "mustachioed devil"—and the first dog alphabetically in the AKC	AFFENPINSCHER (4)
Big black water dog from Canada	NEWFOUNDLAND (3)
Scottish or West Highland White _____	TERRIER (3)
Opposite of Alpha	OMEGA (3)
Extroverted; likes people (a good trait in a therapy dog)	FRIENDLY (2)
Not closed	OPEN (2)
Labrador or Golden _____	RETRIEVER (3)
Dane _____	GREAT (1)
_____ Greyhound (small sight hound in the Toy Group)	ITALIAN (4)
Hungarian pointing dog	VISZLA (2)
Companion Dog _____ (advanced obedience title)	EXCELLENT (3)
Smallest dog breed (from Mexico)	CHIHUAHUA (3)
Sport in which dogs run through an obstacle course	AGILITY (4)
Santa wants to know: Is your dog _____ or nice?	NAUGHTY (2)
An animal's natural behavior	INSTINCT (2)
The name of the dog in "Peter Pan"	NANA (2)
Extremely tiring	EXHAUSTING (3)

Raindog Puzzle II

In this puzzle, the letters from above fall (like raindrops) to the squares directly below them, but must be rearranged. When you fill out the puzzle correctly, you'll have a clever quotation about dogs. (The author of the quotation is listed below the puzzle.)

Hints for solving: Look for single-letter words to start—those are always "A" or "I." Three-letter words are most often "THE" or "DOG."

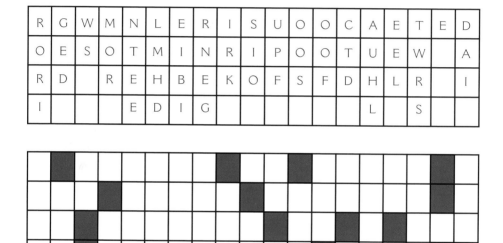

R	G	W	M	N	L	E	R	I	S	U	O	O	C	A	E	T	E	D
O	E	S	O	T	M	I	N	R	I	P	O	O	T	U	E	W		A
R	D		R	E	H	B	E	K	O	F	S	F	D	H	L	R		I
I			E	D	I	G							L		S			

Rita Rudner

Solution: I wonder if other dogs think poodles are members of a weird religious cult.

Substitution Toys

This is a simple substitution code puzzle. Each letter of the alphabet has been replaced by another. Pick the right letters, and you'll decipher the names of nine popular toy breeds.

A Z Z O W P

A P V T Y R P D P

A F R

A Z X P C L Y T L Y

A L A T W W Z Y

N S T S F L S F L

X L W E P D P

J Z C V D S T C P   E P C C T P C

D S T S   E K F

Tracking Puzzle I

Your dog can put his nose down and sniff his way to the answer. Let's see if you can do as well. Follow the word path through to the end. The first letter of the next word is next to the last letter of the previous word—either next to it or below it. To help, we've highlighted the first letter of each new word in yellow. Follow our quotation to the end, and you'll learn some tracking wisdom.

Start Here!

X	Y	**W**	U	T	Y	Y	W	D	G	F	V	G	X	V	E	Q	E	K	M
M	O	H	T	P	W	M	Q	I	M	F	U	V	O	Q	M	M	K	U	E
Y	N	E	Q	U	X	V	K	M	K	W	E	S	G	F	E	L	K	X	O
W	Q	N	**T**	R	A	C	K	I	N	G	Q	W	M	X	G	M	X	M	E
M	U	G	X	G	W	G	X	K	F	**T**	F	L	A	F	W	I	G	E	Z
U	E	U	Q	S	A	M	F	U	F	H	Y	Q	F	Y	M	U	M	K	U
M	Q	K	W	Q	W	V	Q	M	R	E	**N**	O	S	E	**K**	X	N	G	Q
U	E	E	S	K	Y	K	E	Y	M	W	V	V	Q	X	N	V	E	N	I
E	W	G	W	A	W	G	V	G	O	C	M	M	X	H	O	Y	G	R	Q
Q	O	X	X	Q	U	T	M	I	T	U	Y	F	F	Z	W	K	W	Y	K
U	W	G	E	U	E	Q	V	F	F	T	U	M	W	Q	S	**B**	E	S	T

Finish Here!

Answer:

____ _____ ___ ____ _____ ____

Solution:

X	Y	**W**	U	T	Y	Y	W	D	G	F	V	G	X	V	E	Q	E	K	M
M	O	**H**	T	P	W	M	Q	I	M	F	U	V	O	Q	M	M	K	U	E
Y	N	**E**	Q	U	X	V	K	M	K	W	E	S	G	F	E	L	K	X	O
W	Q	**N**	**T**	**R**	**A**	**C**	**K**	**I**	**N**	**G**	Q	W	M	X	G	M	X	M	E
M	U	G	X	G	W	G	X	K	F	**T**	F	L	A	F	W	I	G	E	Z
U	E	U	Q	S	A	M	F	U	F	**H**	Y	Q	F	Y	M	U	M	K	U
M	Q	K	W	Q	W	V	Q	M	R	**E**	**N**	**O**	**S**	**E**	**K**	X	N	G	Q
U	E	E	S	K	Y	K	E	Y	M	W	V	V	Q	X	**N**	V	E	N	I
E	W	G	W	A	W	G	V	G	O	C	M	M	X	H	**O**	Y	G	R	Q
Q	O	X	X	Q	U	T	M	I	T	U	Y	F	F	Z	**W**	K	W	Y	K
U	W	G	E	U	E	Q	V	F	F	T	U	M	W	Q	**S**	**B**	**E**	**S**	**T**

Answer: WHEN TRACKING THE NOSE KNOWS BEST

Tracking Puzzle II

Your dog can put his nose down and sniff his way to the answer. Let's see if you can do as well. Follow the word path through to the end. The first letter of the next word is next to the last letter of the previous word—either next to it or below it. To help, we've highlighted the first letter of each new word in yellow. Follow our quotation to the end, and you'll learn some tracking wisdom.

Start Here!

E	M	E	Q	A	G	S	S	L	M	S	R	N	O	F	U	N	T	Z	T	T	H	E	K
I	L	H	D	X	A	W	O	R	G	G	H	L	Z	E	S	F	E	D	M	E	I	M	G
T	T	I	M	H	A	F	M	T	H	F	Z	I	U	Z	E	D	B	B	C	U	Z	I	M
W	A	T	C	V	I	Z	E	S	A	Y	A	N	H	F	T	R	E	A	L	D	N	G	C
L	O	Z	W	H	A	D	F	K	I	P	T	U	T	T	T	I	N	S	I	N	Z	E	E
M	O	W	F	T	H	I	W	N	T	S	R	M	U	C	D	S	T	O	B	A	T	H	I
N	S	D	E	R	A	L	Z	W	E	B	A	X	X	T	Y	U	H	E	R	F	A	B	U
T	S	T	H	W	D	E	T	Z	A	T	C	I	M	O	N	I	T	Z	C	H	A	G	G
M	E	Y	O	W	N	R	H	S	W	A	K	C	B	I	B	M	A	S	S	Y	P	L	A
K	T	H	S	T	T	L	Y	B	T	R	I	O	E	W	Q	Z	T	E	W	A	Z	X	B
Z	C	B	M	L	J	G	D	S	A	Q	N	R	W	T	Q	A	S	H	E	D	T	H	U
M	N	D	I	T	O	C	D	A	T	W	G	D	O	G	I	Z	E	R	W	Q	I	G	K
D	A	L	L	U	N	O	W	W	Q	E	R	Y	W	Q	S	H	E	A	V	E	N	W	P
C	H	P	H	I	R	U	V	U	E	P	U	W	M	Z	L	U	P	L	U	W	S	U	O
A	O	I	E	Y	E	Y	O	P	Z	S	F	M	S	M	E	S	L	E	E	Z	C	Q	L
N	Y	Y	D	U	S	R	P	W	M	W	D	L	D	F	W	F	P	E	W	P	E	Z	Y
R	R	Q	W	T	D	E	W	F	E	D	E	Z	E	P	Z	D	F	M	Y	E	N	U	W
E	D	T	E	E	Z	D	Y	U	F	M	Z	U	D	E	P	S	F	S	S	W	T	Y	N

Finish Here!

Answer:

____ ___ _ _____ ___ __ _____ _____

Solution:

E	M	E	Q	A	G	S	**S**	L	M	S	R	N	O	F	U	N	T	Z	T	T	H	E	K
I	L	H	D	X	A	W	**O**	R	G	G	H	L	Z	E	S	F	E	D	M	E	I	M	G
T	T	I	M	H	A	F	**M**	T	H	F	Z	I	U	Z	E	D	B	B	C	U	Z	I	M
W	A	T	C	V	I	Z	**E**	**S**	**A**	**Y**	**A**	N	H	F	T	R	E	A	L	D	N	G	C
L	O	Z	W	H	A	D	F	K	I	P	**T**	U	T	T	T	I	N	S	I	N	Z	E	E
M	O	W	F	T	H	I	W	N	T	S	**R**	M	U	C	D	S	T	O	B	A	T	H	I
N	S	D	E	R	A	L	Z	W	E	B	**A**	X	X	T	Y	U	H	E	R	F	A	B	U
T	S	T	H	W	D	E	T	Z	A	T	**C**	I	M	O	N	I	T	Z	C	H	A	G	G
M	E	Y	O	W	N	R	H	S	W	A	**K**	C	B	I	B	M	A	S	S	Y	P	L	A
K	T	H	S	T	T	L	Y	B	T	R	**I**	O	E	W	Q	Z	T	E	W	A	Z	X	B
Z	C	B	M	L	J	G	D	S	A	Q	**N**	R	W	T	Q	A	S	H	E	D	T	H	U
M	N	D	I	T	O	C	D	A	T	W	**G**	**D**	**O**	**G**	**I**	Z	E	R	W	Q	I	G	K
D	A	L	L	U	N	O	W	W	Q	E	R	Y	W	Q	**S**	**H**	**E**	**A**	**V**	**E**	**N**	W	P
C	H	P	H	I	R	U	V	U	E	P	U	W	M	Z	L	U	P	L	U	W	**S**	U	O
A	O	I	E	Y	E	Y	O	P	Z	S	F	M	S	M	E	S	L	E	E	Z	**C**	Q	L
N	Y	Y	D	U	S	R	P	W	M	W	D	L	D	F	W	F	P	E	W	P	**E**	Z	Y
R	R	Q	W	T	D	E	W	F	E	D	E	Z	E	P	Z	D	F	M	Y	E	**N**	U	W
E	D	T	E	E	Z	D	Y	U	F	M	Z	U	D	E	P	S	F	S	S	W	**T**	Y	N

Answer: SOME SAY A TRACKING DOG IS HEAVEN-"SCENT"

Raindog Puzzle III

In this puzzle, the letters from above fall (like raindrops) to the squares directly below them, but must be rearranged. When you fill out the puzzle correctly, you'll have a clever quotation about dogs. (The author of the quotation is listed below the puzzle.)

Hints for solving: Look for single-letter words to start—those are always "A" or "I." Three-letter words are most often "THE" or "DOG."

T	O	N	G	A	V	P	N	A	E	E	E	P	A	G
S	I	S		T	H	A	I	R	S	R	N	D	E	R
E	H	A		A		N	E	C	T	H			O	V
	R	S		E		E	R		G	O				

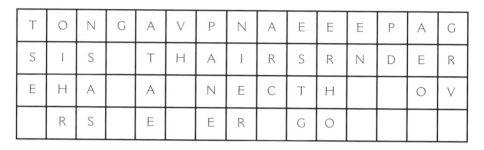

Andy Rooney

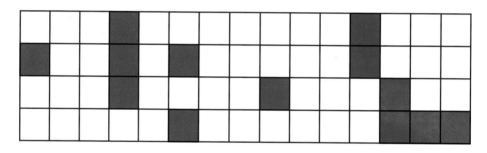

Unearth the Answer!

This puzzle is easy, it just takes a little digging. Cross off the words that are indicated below. The remaining ten words, read left to write, will form a saying about small dogs.

1. Cross off all dog breeds
2. Cross off all dog tricks/commands
3. Cross off all synonyms for "little"
4. Cross off all words that end in the letters "OUGH"
5. Cross off all dog toys
6. Cross off the names of dog-loving countries
7. Cross off all the words that begin and end with the letter "D"
8. Cross off all words that begin and end with the letter "T"
9. Cross off all colors

POODLE	THROUGH	SMALL	FRANCE	DIMINUTIVE
BALL	A	SIT	BEAGLE	BELGIUM
DEED	ENOUGH	TALENT	DISCOVERED	TREAT
FETCH	FRISBEE	DOG	TEENY	IS
TOT	DACHSHUND	RED	WHITE	HEEL
MEASURED	TINY	TOUGH	BY	BLUE
JAPAN	THE	POMERANIAN	DARED	SIZE
STAY	DREAMED	ENGLAND	BEG	THOUGH
OF	SCHNAUZER	WEE	HIS	TOOT
PINK	DID	SILVER	CANADA	HEART

ANSWER: A DOG IS MEASURED BY THE SIZE OF HIS HEART

Solution:

1. POODLE, BEAGLE, DACHSHUND, POMERANIAN, SCHNAUZER
2. SIT, FETCH, HEEL, STAY, BEG
3. SMALL, DIMINUTIVE, TEENY, TINY, WEE
4. ENOUGH, TOUGH, THOUGH, THROUGH
5. BALL, FRISBEE
6. FRANCE, BELGIUM, JAPAN, ENGLAND, CANADA
7. DEED, DARED, DID, DISCOVERED, DREAMED
8. TALENT, TREAT, TOT, TOOT
9. RED, WHITE, BLUE, PINK, SILVER

Raindog Puzzle IV

In this puzzle, the letters from above fall (like raindrops) to the squares directly below them, but must be rearranged. When you fill out the puzzle correctly, you'll have a clever quotation about dogs. (The author of the quotation is listed below the puzzle.)

Hints for solving: Look for single-letter words to start—those are always "A" or "I." Three-letter words are most often "THE" or "DOG."

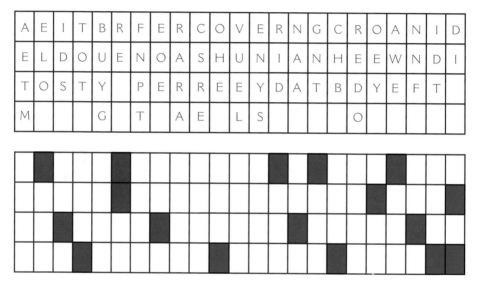

A	E	I	T	B	R	F	E	R	C	O	V	E	R	N	G	C	R	O	A	N	I	D
E	L	D	O	U	E	N	O	A	S	H	U	N	I	A	N	H	E	E	W	N	D	I
T	O	S	T	Y		P	E	R	R	E	E	Y	D	A	T	B	D	Y	E	F	T	
M			G		T		A	E		L		S				O						

Robert Benchley

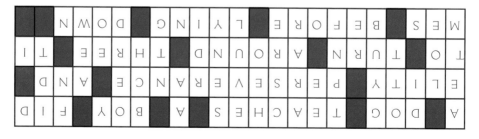

Agility Word Seek Puzzle

To solve this puzzle, you must have an agile mind! Circle the letters in the words listed below the puzzle. The remaining letters, read from left to right, will spell out a word that describes agility competitors!

The solution has 8 letters.

H	U	R	D	L	E	S	E	L	D	O	O	P	E	A
E	D	S	S	P	E	E	D	Y	E	A	R	U	C	T
I	N	P	Q	U	A	L	I	F	Y	I	N	G	R	E
G	O	I	N	G	C	O	M	P	E	T	I	T	O	R
H	B	N	J	U	M	P	I	N	G	H	L	A	F	O
T	I	M	E	S	F	E	D	O	G	W	A	L	K	S
N	A	D	A	C	U	V	F	L	A	S	H	K	C	E
B	A	R	K	U	S	A	A	F	R	A	M	E	I	P
T	P	E	E	T	S	E	S	L	E	N	N	U	T	A
E	N	I	L	E	E	W	A	Y	L	I	P	P	A	H
G	N	I	T	N	A	P	A	P	I	L	L	O	N	S
C	L	A	P	P	I	N	G	N	I	N	N	I	W	A
F	U	N	N	Y	R	A	L	U	P	O	P	I	W	R
P	E	K	I	N	G	E	S	E	E	T	F	L	A	B
L	A	U	G	H	I	N	G	E	S	T	O	U	G	H

Solution: ATHLETES

AFRAME BARK BOND BRASH CLAPPING COMPETITOR
CUTE DOGWALK FLAB FLASH FLY FORCE FUNNY FUSS
GOING HAPPILY HEIGHT HURDLES JUMPING LAUGHING
LEEWAY LINE NADAC PANTING PAPILLONS PAWS
PEKINGESE PINT POODLES POPULAR PUG (find it twice)
QUALIFYING SHAPES SORE SPEEDY STEEP SPIN SWIFT
TALK TICK TIMES TOUGH TUNNELS WAG WEAVE POLES
WINNING USA YEAR

Appendix

The Basic Commands

This is a summary of some of the basic that will help you and your dog in the activities in this book. This summary gives a quick lesson on how to teach the command in a way that most dogs will understand.

For a more detailed approach, as well as information on solving behavior problems, take a look at *Little Dogs: Training Your Pint-Sized Companion*, the companion volume to this book.

Watch Me!

The "Watch Me" command is makes all other obedience infinitely easier to teach. A dog who is looking at you is more likely to learn what you are teaching him, just as kids in school are more likely to learn when they watch their teacher.

To teach "Watch Me":

1. Hold a treat between your eyes and say "Watch me." The dog will stare at you longingly. Well, he'll stare at the treat, but since the treat is between your eyes, he'll be focusing in your direction.
2. Instantly say, "Good watch me!" and reward the dog with the treat.
3. After the dog is looking at you consistently, hold the treat in your hand (out of sight of the dog).
4. Say "watch me."
5. If he looks at you, say "Good watch me!" and reward him.
6. If he looks at your hand, say "uh-uh, watch me." When he looks at your face, reward him.
8. If he doesn't understand, then hold the treat in front of your eyes again, and remind him of what you want.
9. Mix up holding treats in front of your eyes and having a treat in your hand until you eventually always have the treat in your hand.

10. Over time, require the dog to look at you for longer periods of time before giving the reward.

Practice "watch me" several times a day, always with a food reward!

Sit!

This is the easiest method to teach "sit," and is perfect for every well-behaved pet.

1. Hold a treat in front of your dog's nose.
2. Slowly pull the treat over the dog's head, between the dog's ears. Almost all dogs will naturally "rock" back into a sit.
3. Say "good sit!" and give the reward *while the dog is in the sitting position.*
4. If the dog doesn't automatically sit, *gently* tuck your finger under his rear to help him go into a "sit" position.
5. If your dog is turning around, you might want to practice in a confined space. Put him on a comfortable chair where he feels safe. He'll back up to the back of the chair, and then you can lure him into a sit.
6. If you notice that your dog is doing a "sit up and beg" position that means you're holding the treat too high. Hold it just above his nose.

Important: Don't EVER push down on your dog's rear end to make him sit. It can damage any dog—and can easily permanently injure a small breed puppy's hips and back! Don't ever pinch his kidneys (as some trainers show you), as this can potentially harm him internally.

Let the treat do the work. Your dog will figure it out. Just be patient, and let him take his time.

Stay!

Be sure your dog knows and understands "sit" before you start. "Sit" and "stay" are two different commands.

1. After you tell your dog "sit" take a step back about 6 inches and gently say "Stay, good sit-stay."
2. *Instantly* and *while he is still sitting* reward him. He can't learn to sit for one minute until he's learned to sit for one second.
3. When he succeeds at a one-second sit-stay, expand the time to 5 seconds, 10 seconds, etc.
4. If he consistently gets up after (for example) 15 seconds, give him a 12 second "stay" and reward him. Help him succeed.
5. Chain together two or more "stays." Tell him "stay" and reward after 10 seconds, then step back and tell him "stay" and reward him after another 15 seconds.
6. Keep your tone happy! This isn't punishment—it's fun. There's no need to make "stay" anything but a fun accomplishment for your dog.

7. When your dog is doing a sit-stay *reward him while he's in the stay position*! The dog will understand much more quickly what you want him to do, and he will quickly become patient, waiting for the reward he knows will be coming to him if he stays still. If you reward a dog consistently while he stays still, then he'll learn to love to do a sit-stay.

Come!

"Come" needs to be taught in an enclosed room or a completely fenced-in area. Put your dog on a long leash—but only use it to corral him if he decides to go running and circles and play "zoomies." DON"T pull on the leash when you teach him this fun, energetic, lively command.

For the first few weeks, teaching "come" is a two person job. Someone else needs to hold the dog while you walk away and call the dog. (If you're both in the same household, it's great to call the dog back and forth.) The person holding the dog should be *silent*.

You should get the dog revved up, eager to come to you, so in a high, happy voice, say, "Ready? Ready? Ready?"

3. Call him with a very clear "come!" command.
4. Be very, very fun. Use a happy voice. Squat down and clap your hands, or turn and run the other direction. Make yourself interesting and appealing.
6. When your dog comes to you, treat him and praise him for *at least 15 seconds*. Your dog needs to know that you're excited that he came to you—so act like it!

Practice three times a day. Don't over-do this one, since you want to keep this a spontaneous, joyful communication between you and your dog.

Down

The dog should be standing and relaxed. Most books and trainers will tell you to teach "down" from a sit. Dogs who have recently learned to "sit" and "stay" are terribly confused when suddenly you're telling them to "down." If you start from a standing position, they're much less worried when learning this exercise.

1. Hold a treat between your dog's front toes
2. He'll reach down for the treat and may drop in a "down" position.
3. Say "Good Down!" and give him the treat!
4. If he doesn't drop, keep the treat on the floor, pushing it slightly toward his chest. If he physically follows the treat with his nose, his chest will go down on the ground.
5. Say "Good Down" and reward him when his chest rests on the ground.

Be patient. Sometimes it takes some maneuvering before your dog learns to "down." If he's getting frustrated, reward partial success. So, if his chest is on the ground but his rear end is still high in the air, give him a treat with a "Yes!" for the partial success. Build on the partial success until he downs with his whole body—at which time say

"Good Down" and treat him generously.

The Down-Stay

Once your dog is comfortable doing a down, it's time to add "Stay." Teach this exactly the way you taught the sit-stay.

1. After you tell your dog "down" take a step back about 6 inches and gently say "Stay, good down-stay." 2. *Instantly* and *while he is still in the down position* reward him.
3. When he succeeds at a one-second down-stay, expand the time to 5 seconds, 10 seconds, etc.
4. If he consistently gets up after (for example) 15 seconds, give him a 12 second "stay" and reward him.
5. Chain together two or more "stays." Tell him "stay" and reward after 10 seconds, then step back and tell him "stay" and reward him after another 15 seconds.

Walking On a Loose Leash

Your dog should be on a comfortable buckle or snap collar (*not a choke collar*) or a harness. Have him on a light-weight four-foot or six-foot leash (*not a flexi leash*).

1. Say, "Let's go" (or "walkies" or whatever word suits you) and start walking.
2. If he pulls, turn the other direction and say "Let's go!" the instant his leash tightens.
3. If he runs out and pulls in the new direction, turn and go a different way, saying, "Let's go!"
4. The moment he's walking on a loose leash, give him (an easily chewed) treat, and tell him he's a very, very good dog.

Very quickly, your dog will figure out that he will never, ever get where he wants to go if he pulls. On the other hand, keeping an eye on you is incredibly fun. Soon, he will be merrily walking on a loose leash!

Release!

One of the hardest things is for a dog to know when a command is over. Teach your dog a release word. When you say this word, your dog's exercise is finished. He can relax and do whatever he wants to do—or whatever you ask next. Any word or short phrase will do: "At ease!", "Your done!", "Off duty!", "Free Dog!", or "That'll do." *Don't* use a word you commonly use in conversation, such as "Okay."
Don't use "Good!" or other words of praise as your release word. (You want to tell your dog he's good in the middle of an exercise—and still have him continue to stay, come, or sit. The release word must be separate and distinct in sound from "Good!") Be sure to give your dog his release word at the end of every exercise, so he knows when it's done. Clarity will help him do a better job!

Resources

Organizations

Adoption and Rescue

American Humane Association (AHA)
63 Inverness Drive East
Englewood, CO 80112
Telephone: (303) 792-9900
Fax: 792-5333
www.americanhumane.org

American Society for the Prevention of Cruelty to Animals (ASPCA)
424 E. 92nd Street
New York, NY 10128-6804
Telephone: (212) 876-7700
www.aspca.org

The Humane Society of the United States (HSUS)
2100 L Street, NW
Washington DC 20037
Telephone: (202) 452-1100
www.hsus.org

Royal Society for the Prevention of Cruelty to Animals (RSPCA)
Telephone: 0870 3335 999
Fax: 0870 7530 284
www.rspca.org.uk

Clubs

American Kennel Club (AKC)
5580 Centerview Drive
Raleigh, NC 27606
Telephone: (919) 233-9767
Fax: (919) 233-3627
E-mail: info@akc.org
www.akc.org

Canadian Kennel Club (CKC)
89 Skyway Avenue, Suite 100
Etobicoke, Ontario M9W 6R4
Telephone: (416) 675-5511
Fax: (416) 675-6506
E-mail: information@ckc.ca
www.ckc.ca

Federation Cynologique Internationale (FCI)
Secretariat General de la FCI
Place Albert 1er, 13
B – 6530 Thuin
Belqique
www.fci.be

The Kennel Club
1 Clarges Street
London
W1J 8AB
Telephone: 0870 606 6750
Fax: 0207 518 1058
www.the-kennel-club.org.uk

United Kennel Club (UKC)
100 E. Kilgore Road
Kalamazoo, MI 49002-5584
Telephone: (269) 343-9020
Fax: (269) 343-7037
E-mail: pbickell@ukcdogs.com
www.ukcdogs.com

Health

Academy of Veterinary Homeopathy (AVH)
P.O. Box 9280
Wilmington, DE 19809
Telephone: (866) 652-1590
Fax: (866) 652-1590
E-mail: office@TheAVH.org
www.theavh.org

American Holistic Veterinary Medical Association (AHVMA)
2218 Old Emmorton Road
Bel Air, MD 21015
Telephone: (410) 569-0795
Fax: (410) 569-2346
E-mail: office@ahvma.org
www.ahvma.org

American Veterinary Chiropractic Association
442154 E 140 Road
Bluejacket, Oklahoma 74333
Telephone: (918) 784-2231
Fax: (918) 784-2675
E-mail: amvetchiro@aol.com
www.animalchiropractic.org

American Veterinary Medical Association (AVMA)
1931 North Meacham Road – Suite 100
Schaumburg, IL 60173
Telephone: (847) 925-8070
Fax: (847) 925-1329
E-mail: avmainfo@avma.org
www.avma.org

ASPCA Animal Poison Control Center
1717 South Philo Road, Suite 36
Urbana, IL 61802
Telephone: (888) 426-4435
www.aspca.org

International Veterinary Acupuncture Society
PO Box 271395
Ft. Collins, CO 80527-1395
Telephone: (970) 266-0666
Fax: (970) 266-0777
www.ivas.org

Northwest School of Animal Massage
PO Box 670
Fall City. WA 98024
Telephone: (877) 836-3703
Fax: (425) 222-4573
www.nwsam.com.

Pet Sitters

National Association of Professional Pet Sitters
15000 Commerce Parkway, Suite C
Mt. Laurel, NJ 08054
Telephone: (800) 296-PETS
Fax: (856) 439-0525
E-mail: napps@ahint.com
www.petsitters.org

Pet Sitters International
201 East King Street
King, NC 27021-9161
Telephone: (336) 983-9222
Fax: (336) 983-5266
E-mail: info@petsit.com
www.petsit.com

Special Needs

Deaf Dog Education Action Fund
P.O. Box 2840
Oneco, FL 34264-2840
www.deafdogs.org

Sports

International Agility Link (IAL)
Global Administrator: Steve Drinkwater
E-mail: yunde@powerup.au
www.agilityclick.com/~ial

North American Dog Agility Council
11522 South Hwy 3
Cataldo, ID 83810
www.nadac.com

North American Flyball Association
1400 West Devon Avenue, #512
Chicago, IL 60660
Phone: 800-318-6312
E-mail: flyball@flyball.org
www.flyball.org.

United States Dog Agility Association
P.O. Box 850955
Richardson, TX 75085-0955
Telephone: (972) 487-2200
www.usdaa.com

World Canine Freestyle Organization
P.O. Box 350122
Brooklyn, NY 11235-2525
Phone: 718-0332-8336
Fax: 7180646-2686
E-mail: wcfodogs@aol.com
www.worldcaninefreestyle.org.

Therapy
Delta Society
875 124th Ave NE, Suite 101
Bellevue, WA 98005
Telephone: (425) 226-7357
Fax: (425) 235-1076
E-mail: info@deltasociety.org
www.deltasociety.org

Therapy Dogs, Inc.
P.O. Box 5868
Cheyenne, WY 82003
Phone: 877-843-7364
www.therapydogs.com

Therapy Dogs International (TDI)
88 Bartley Road
Flanders, NJ 07836
Telephone: (973) 252-9800
Fax: (973) 252-7171
E-mail: tdi@gti.net
www.tdi-dog.org

Training
Association of Pet Dog Trainers (APDT)
150 Executive Center Drive Box 35
Greenville, SC 29615
Telephone: (800) PET-DOGS
Fax: (864) 331-0767
E-mail: information@apdt.com
www.apdt.com

Publications

Books
Albrecht, Kathy, *The Lost Pet Chronicles: Adventures of a K-9 Cop Turned Pet Detective*, Bloomsbury, 2004.

Becker, Marty, DVM, and Robert Kushner, MD, *Fitness Unleashed! A Dog and Owner's Guide to Losing Weight and Gaining Health Together*, Three Rivers Press, 2006.

Ganz, Sandy and Susan Boyd, *Tracking from the Ground Up*, Show Me Publications, 1992.

Hastings, Pat and Erin Rouse, *Another Piece of the Puzzle: Puppy Development*, Dogfolk, 2004.

Leach, Laurie, *The Beginner's Guide to Dog Agility*, TFH Publications, 2006.

Levin, Caroline D., *Blind Dog Stories: Tales of Triumph, Humor and Heroism*, Lantern Publications, 1999.

Levin, Caroline D., *Living With Blind Dogs: A Resource Book and Training Guide for the Owners of Blind and Low Vision Dogs*, Lantern Publications, 2003.

Sanders, William, *Enthusiastic Tracking: The Step-By-Step Training Manual*, Rime Publications, 1998.

Traveling with Your Pet: The AAA PetBook, AAA Publications, 2001.

Magazines
AKC Family Dog
American Kennel Club
260 Madison Avenue
New York, NY 10016
Telephone: (800) 490-5675
E-mail: familydog@akc.org
www.akc.org/pubs/familydog

AKC Gazette
American Kennel Club
260 Madison Avenue
New York, NY 10016
Telephone: (800) 533-7323
E-mail: gazette@akc.org
www.akc.org/pubs/gazette

Dog & Kennel
Pet Publishing, Inc.
7-L Dundas Circle
Greensboro, NC 27407
Telephone: (336) 292-4272
Fax: (336) 292-4272
E-mail: info@petpublishing.com
www.dogandkennel.com

Dog Fancy
Subscription Department
P.O. Box 53264
Boulder, CO 80322-3264
Telephone: (800) 365-4421
E-mail: barkback@dogfancy.com
www.dogfancy.com

Dogs Monthly
Ascot House
High Street, Ascot,
Berkshire SL5 7JG
United Kingdom
Telephone: 0870 730 8433
Fax: 0870 730 8431
E-mail: admin@rtc-
associates.freeserve.co.uk
www.corsini.co.uk/dogsmonthly

Websites

Agility Ability
www.agilityability.com
Information and tips from agility lovers.

American Border Collie Network
www.abcollie.com
If you want to check out herding trials
with your little dog, the ABCN has lists
of trial dates.

Clean Run
www.cleanrun.com
Sources for magazines, agility training
books, videos, dog training equipment,
and all sorts of products for dog agility
training and trialing, dog obedience
training, flyball training, clicker training,
and just having fun with your dog.

The Dog Agility Page
www.dogpatch.org/agility
Links to just about everything agility-
related on the internet.

Dog Birthdays and Parties
www.dogbirthdaysandparties.com
From dog birthday cakes to gifts and
invitations, everything you need for your
dog birthday party is right here.

GlobalPetFinder
www.globalpetfinder.com
The latest in proven gps and 2-way
wireless technology to help you keep
track of your beloved pet.

Petswelcome
www.petswelcome.com.
Complete listings for 25,000 pet-friendly
hotels, B&Bs, ski resorts, campgrounds,
and beaches.

Ruff Wear
www.ruffwear.com
Gear For Dogs On the Go® combines
performance, quality, fit, function and
safety to meet the needs of active and
adventurous dogs and their companions.

Tail Waggin' Celebrations
www.tailwagging.com
Provides unique, fun party packages and
accessories for your dog and their guests
for any type of celebration.

Tellington TTouch
www.tteam-ttouch.com
Linda Tellington-Jones' website gives a
listing of TTouch practitioners around the
world, and also has books on the subject
for sale.

**University of Tennessee Canine and
Equine Rehabilitation**
www.canineequinerehab.com.
The educational leader in canine and
equine rehabilitation.

Index

Photo Credits

Illustrations

Dedication

Wunsum Bit Lit Golden Girl CD CGC

Goldie, my sweet old girl, you are the dog who changed my life and taught me to find the joy in every day

U-CDX Aranon Music Maestro Please CDX HIC CGC

Radar, you are the dog I dreamed of having since I was 12 years old: smart, loyal, and a lot like a real-life Lassie

La Ren I Go By Pogo CDX CGC Delta Society Pet Partner Therapy Dog

Pogo, you are a dog for the ages: gentle, kind, and so full of life you are almost bursting at the seams

Acknowledgements

First and foremost, thanks to the team at TFH.

Chris Reggio, thanks for asking me to write this book. What a lucky writer I am to be invited into such an entertaining, interesting project. Heather Russell-Revesz, you are the editing goddess. And thank you Mary Ann Kahn for the design and art skills that made this book a pleasure to pick up and read and April Chmura for her lovely and fun illustrations.

I have so many kind and true friends, trainers and teachers who taught me things that are reflected in this book. I hope this book conveys even a sliver of the wisdom and knowledge I've learned from them.

The wonderful Ellie Wyckoff continues to be my inspiration and mentor. Whatever I pass on about respectful, loving, kind training has its roots in what I learn from Ellie every week. Thank you, Ellie, for showing me the way.

I've had the rare privilege of taking musical freestyle classes with Brigitte Sclabas this year. The insights and ideas that are in that chapter come from her wonderful teaching. When she dances with her Poodles, it really is magic.

Joan Armstrong taught me about tracking and rally obedience. She's a great trainer and a brilliant thinker about all things dog.

Susan Fletcher's trick class from several years ago still comes in handy today.

Other friends teach me less formally, but they teach me nonetheless. My great friend Leah Atwood provided the recipes in this book. She's also a fabulous freestyler — so any ideas about dancing with dogs that didn't come from Brigitte came from Leah. She is a dear and true friend.

Lisa Keppinger gave me acupuncture when I needed it most to keep my body together and ideas flowing. While she punctured me, she added ideas for the book. She and her Miniature Dachshunds are powerful healers.